D0088728

# MARRIAGE ANNULMENT
# IN THE
# CATHOLIC CHURCH

A Practical Guide
by
RALPH BROWN

Lexington College

310 S. Peoria St. Ste 512
Chicago, Il 60607 3534

Phone 312-226-6294
Fax    312-226-6405

# KEVIN MAYHEW
## Publishers

First published in Great Britain in 1977 by
KEVIN MAYHEW LTD
55 Leigh Road
Leigh-on-Sea Essex

© Copyright 1977 by Ralph Brown

ISBN 0 905725 10 7

Nihil obstat                          R. J. Cuming, D.D. Censor
Imprimatur                              + Basil Cardinal Hume
Westminster 16.xi.1976

Printed and bound by E. T. Heron & Co. Ltd., Essex and London

262.9

# CONTENTS

# FOREWORD

One of the very heartening features of recent years is the developing interest which is evident on the part of clergy, Religious and the laity in the problems of marriage. No-one, of course, is quite so starry-eyed as to imagine marriage—as any other state of life—does not have its special problems. For a long time interest and deep concern has been shown in these problems by bodies such as the Catholic Marriage Advisory Council. This concern can, of course, only extend to situations in which the problems are soluble. When they are not, then eventually, apart from sympathy and support, such agencies have come to the end of their ability to help, although there remains the role of support. This often means that the outcome of the problem is separation; and frequently in the present day, divorce.

The divorce rate has continued to grow and the rate of growth is alarming, as the Registrar General's Statistical Review for each year very plainly shows. It is not possible to state—as *was* the case—that Catholics are 'not really involved' in this growth rate of divorce figures. There are no reliable statistics to show the proportion of Catholics involved; but reason alone indicates that they cannot be unaffected by this social feature of our present day.

It is at this stage that one of the other agencies of the Church comes into play. This is the Marriage Tribunal, generally centred in each Diocese, though sometimes arranged on a regional basis. This is one of the 'caring agencies' of the Church which is specially commissioned to investigate petitions presented to establish if the parties in question can be allowed to enter further unions; on the basis of an annulment, dispensation of an unconsummated marriage, or a dissolution of a non-sacramental union.

In the past there was a widely held view among Canonists that persons would approach a Marriage Tribunal with the conviction that their marriages were invalid or dissoluble for some reason; and the formal canonical procedure was sometimes commenced to examine this claim. There has been a very radical alteration in the approach of Canonists to this matter over the last ten or so years. They no longer expect people to come along with claims of nullity to be investigated. What in fact happens is that people whose marriages have broken down come to a Tribunal and try to find out if there is anything that can be done to permit them to enter new marriages; or sometimes to see if an existing second union (contracted after the breakdown of the first) can be sacramentalised in the Church.

Although the procedure—now and some years ago—is very similar, what is different is the starting point of Canonists. The starting point now is very much to see if the person in question can be helped (by whatever means) to resume, or enter into or continue his or her life within the Church on a fully sacramental basis. Sometimes this is possible, often it is not. The sphere of action for a Tribunal is fairly restricted. But it is restricted within the confines of what the Church believes marriage to be—essentially a union which is indissoluble, provided it is valid, sacramental and consummated. This book is concerned with those confines within which a Marriage Tribunal has to work.

There are two aspects with which this book deals. One concerns the procedure which must be adopted in the examination of a marriage, its circumstances and the parties to it. The other concerns the law which constitutes the criteria for this examination. Essentially, of course, the law is contained within the *Code of Canon Law*. However, a vast part of the ramifications of what is briefly mentioned in the *Code* is contained in another source—namely the jurisprudence of the Church's courts.

The Church's jurisprudence in the area of marriage is the product of case after case in which the law is explained and refined. Naturally this constant process of explanation and refinement of concepts leads to development; to a greater understanding of what constitutes marriage, especially what creates a bar to a union being a valid marriage. This development of the law is nothing new; it has continued over centuries of the Church's history. Sometimes various aspects of this development may, however, appear to be 'new law'; but this is only because there is a very faulty notion of what 'development' means. And because some people come new to a realisation of the Church's law and its system of jurisprudence.

On the other hand, the Popes have constantly stressed the need for a deeper study of the other-than-theological sciences so that the Church may develop in its pursuit of the truth. It is here that the closer examination of the insights of physical and psychological medicine has been of the greatest help to the Church in its understanding of marriage. For example, the greater knowledge of sexual and psychosexual problems has both been a help in rescuing marriages and in enabling one to see where there was no marriage.

This book is about the procedure by which marriage cases are dealt with; and about the law and jurisprudence which govern the decisions of the Marriage Tribunals. It is not a work for specialists.

Its purpose has been to describe in direct and non-technical language both these elements of a 'marriage-case', so as to help, especially, those unhappily involved in such situations; to give some indication of what is possible; and to give some hope to those who most need it. It cannot be claimed that every broken marriage situation is amenable to Tribunal help. Indeed, sadly, it is by no means the bulk of such cases which can be assisted. For those others who cannot be helped, however, often a Tribunal is the first step in the direction of some form of pastoral help, counselling and support for such, often, apparently intolerable situations.

Readers will be aware that the present *Code of Canon Law* is under revision. The finalised version of a new Code, however, is unlikely to be promulgated for some years. But it is possible to state that already a large number of variations of the originally published Code of 1918 have been built into the current procedure for marriage cases. The future Code will merely incorporate these variations into the appropriate sections; so that it is more than likely that the procedure (not the jurisprudence) will remain substantially as it is today. The jurisprudence will, of course, continue to develop.

This is the third edition of a book which was originally published in 1970. The second edition was basically the same as the first but for the addition of a special appendix on certain modifications of the procedure which had been introduced in such places as Canada and the United States. This third edition is, however, substantially different from the first two editions. All the procedural alterations in Tribunal work have been incorporated; but more important, the jurisprudential developments of the last fifteen years have also been included under their appropriate sections. It is these jurisprudential advances which it is hoped will give most help to persons who are struggling with the trauma of a broken marriage. In any event, it is the hope that whoever reads this book will receive help in his or her individual situation; whether hope for a person with a broken marriage; or help for a Priest, Nun, Brother, Counsellor or Teacher in dealing with special cases, or imparting the good news of the work of the caring Church. If the final situation is one where the grace of God can be recognised, the mercy of God received or the help of God discovered, then whatever work has gone into writing the book will have been amply rewarded.

No book of this sort is written in a vacuum. It is written as the result of experience gained and insights received. In this area I have as a debt of honour as well as friendship to offer my deep personal thanks to two colleagues—Edward Dunderdale and Michael Ashdowne—whose friendship, wise guidance and brilliant ideas have been a source of inspiration to me and formed the background to what I know of Canon Law, both practical and theoretical. I must also thank Kevin Mayhew for his help and encouragement; and finally, but by no means last in order of gratitude, I must thank Dorothy Grey and Veronica Mars who prepared the typescript.

42 Francis Street                                              Ralph Brown
LONDON SW1
1 October 1976

# Chapter 1

# THE SCOPE OF MARRIAGE TRIBUNAL WORK

Part of the Catholic Church's teaching on marriage is that a valid, sacramental and consummated union is indissoluble. This has been the pattern of the Church's teaching for centuries. What this means is that two baptized persons, who are married in accordance with the law, and whose union has been consummated, are bound in an indissoluble union sanctified by God until the death of one of the partners. This applies equally to Catholics and non-Catholics. The only additional law to which Catholics must conform is the rule of the Church that, without a general or special dispensation, those baptized in the Catholic Church must be married before a priest and two witnesses. This additional rule is termed the form of marriage and applies throughout the Latin Church, but for special reasons it can be dispensed. With such a dispensation a Catholic is permitted to contract marriage validly and lawfully in a church and before the minister of another denomination. There has also been a general dispensation from the form of marriage which permits Catholics to be married to members of the Orthodox Church in the church of their partner. The teaching that a valid, sacramental and con-summated union is indissoluble until death is true even of a marriage between two non-Catholics which takes place in church or in a register office.

It is often thought, both by Catholics and non-Catholics alike, that the Church does not recognize marriages which take place between two non-Catholics in a register office. As we have said above, this is not the case. Apart from the case of Catholics who are bound to the form of marriage, a marriage can (canonically) take place anywhere. The Church teaches that what makes the marriage is the consent of the partners. Assuming that consent has been given by both the parties to a marriage, the union is valid. Moreover, assuming that this same union is also sacramental and con-summated, it is indissoluble.

It will be seen that the Church stresses the three elements of an indissoluble union, namely validity, sacramentality and con-summation. But, although a union which enjoys these three elements is indissoluble, it also follows that a union which does not possess these three qualities may be, in some sense of the word, dissoluble; or may be said not to exist. The work of a marriage tribunal centres around the determination of these three elements: whether the marriage is invalid; whether it is non-sacramental; whether it is unconsummated. The next few pages will be devoted to an examination of what is meant by the three terms validity, sacramentality and consummation.

## I  VALIDITY

For a considerable period within the history of the Church there was some debate as to precisely what made a marriage. One view, held by the school of law of Bologna, maintained that the element which made the marriage was consummation. The opposing view, held by the law school of Paris, maintained that it was consent which made the marriage valid. Although this was a somewhat rarified debate, the two views were reflected by the teaching of the scholars of the two universities. However, the debate was resolved during the reign of Pope Alexander III (1159-1181), when the Pope declared for the side which seemed to him to bear the weight of tradition; and from this time onwards the authoritative teaching in the Church was that consent makes the marriage.

A Christian marriage involves a union 'which has been established by God and qualified by his laws. It is rooted in the conjugal covenant of irrevocable personal consent. Hence, by that human act whereby the spouses mutually bestow and accept each other, a relationship arises by the Divine Will which, in the eyes of society too, is a lasting one' (Pastoral Constitution of the Second Vatican Council: *The Church in the Modern World* §48). This description of marriage is deeply impressive; it is couched in language which is pastoral and real, rather than dry and legal. Nonetheless, the description contains a number of very precise notions which must here be mentioned. Irrevocable personal consent is given by the two parties to a union involving a relationship between them which is lasting and permanent. There is a mutual giving or exchange which involves the couple in a permanence that is foreseen and strengthened by the Divine Will. The clear meaning here is that this union forged by the consent of the parties is irrevocable and lasting, permanent 'until death do us part'.

But, in addition, the same Conciliar document goes on to state that, 'By their very nature, the institution of matrimony and conjugal love are ordained for the procreation and education of children . . .' (*The Church in the Modern World*, ibid). The Council is here stating nothing more than that one of the purposes of the conjugal state is the children that may come forth from the union.

But there is no compulsion about having children; merely a statement that this is one of the purposes of the bond. This portion of the text must be taken together with the one mentioned earlier, both of which underline that there is a free giving of consent, an exchange, to a union which in no way excludes the possibility of children. It is also implicit here that each of the parties, as a result of the consent freely given and accepted, is entitled to be a parent.

The Constitution goes on, in the next paragraph, to state: 'Thus a man and a woman who, by the marriage covenant of conjugal love "are no longer two, but one flesh", render mutual help and service to each other through an intimate union of their persons and of their actions . . . . As a mutual gift of two persons, this intimate union, as well as the good of the children, imposes total fidelity on the spouses and argues for an unbreakable oneness between them' (*The Church in the Modern World*, ibid). The teaching here is that the married state, because of the consent given by the parties to each other and because of their rights to children, also imposes upon the couple the obligation of total fidelity so as to safeguard the union and the children of the union.

These three points, made so clearly by the Constitution on *The Church in the Modern World*, are basic essentials of Christian marriage, namely the permanence of the bond, the right to children within the union, and the total fidelity imposed on the couple as a result of the other two essentials. This is what a couple consent to when they exchange their promises in marriage. It is evident that some persons can enter into a state which could loosely be called marriage because the parties do all the necessary external things that they are called upon to do by the laws of the Church. It is however, possible to conceive of a situation when the person, although not forced into marriage, is put into a position where, though he cannot escape from the forthcoming union, he does not want to contract the marriage. He could, although expressing all the external signs of consent, completely refuse his consent to the union. If this were the case, the marriage would not be valid; it would not exist, since the person concerned has not 'consented to Christian marriage'. The union would be null and void because of the total lack of his consent.

Again, the consent required to make the marriage is the consent of a human being. If a person goes through the outward form of the marriage bereft of his senses, this could not be classified as a human act. Thus insanity would prevent a person from giving proper consent to a marriage, and a union entered into by a person who is shown to be insane at the time would not be a Christian marriage. *The Church in the Modern World* also refers to the exchange of

consent giving rise to a 'relationship'. There can be situations where
a person is totally incapable of forming such a married relationship.
If the inability to form such a relationship can be proved (leaving
aside for the moment the matter of proof), the union would also be
null and void.

We have already mentioned the case of the person who enters into
a union, but because of his total lack of consent, the union cannot be
described as a Christian marriage. There are other circumstances in
which, although a person does give his consent to a Christian
marriage, the consent given is not free. Although the actual and
necessary consent has been given to this union, the Church
legislates (as she has power to do in respect of marriage) that where
consent is obtained as a result of force exerted and fear induced, the
resulting union would be regarded as null and void.

All the elements which have been mentioned above are ones
which have to be most carefully considered by a tribunal. Each of
them, namely complete lack of consent to a Christian marriage,
exclusion of the permanence of marriage, the exclusion of the right
to children, the exclusion of fidelity, the inability to consent, or
consent obtained as a result of grave pressure will be examined
further in Chapter Two.

*The Church in the Modern World* restates that marriage has been
established by God and 'qualified by his laws'. When Christ
founded his Church, he committed into the hands of Peter and the
Apostles the guardianship of the Sacraments within the Church. It
is from this that the Church derives her power to legislate upon the
Sacraments. It is this reason that allows the Church to establish
certain laws concerning the existence and contracting of marriage.
Certain laws of the Church on marriage are of the greatest
importance. Some of these laws are called Divine Laws, insofar as it
is considered that they have been established by God, and are
merely restated by the Church. Other laws concerning marriage are
ones which have been made by the Church; these are called
ecclesiastical laws. Thus some laws prevent a valid marriage taking
place: for example it is not possible for a boy to marry his mother or
his sister. Such prohibitions are considered to be of the Divine Law.
Another law, usually regarded as being of ecclesiastical origin,
forbids two first cousins marrying. When the laws which the
Church has either restated from the Divine Law, or formulated as
ecclesiastical law, prohibit marriage either absolutely or less
severely, such laws are termed impediments. Some of these
impediments are of such a kind that if a marriage takes place in spite
of them, and without sanction of the Church, the marriage will be
invalid. There are others of slightly lesser importance which do not

invalidate a marriage, but which nonetheless must be observed under pain of serious offence against God. Some of these impediments can be dispensed (those of ecclesiastical origin), and some cannot be dispensed (those of divine origin).

A marriage tribunal is greatly concerned with all these impediments. Generally speaking, the matters which concern consent or the lack of it are dealt with by what is termed *formal nullity procedure*. Other matters concerning impediments and whether they have been dispensed or not, are usually dealt with under the heading of an *informal nullity procedure*. We will turn to these matters in the next chaper. For the present it is merely stated that matters concerning consent and impediments are the subject of *nullity cases*.

## II  SACRAMENTALITY

In speaking about the married state, the Constitution *The Church in the Modern World* says: 'Authentic married love is caught up into divine love and is governed and enriched by Christ's redeeming power and the saving activity of the Church. This love can lead the spouses to God with powerful effect and can aid and strengthen them in the sublime office of being father or mother.' The married state is being spoken of here as the means by which a couple can fulfil their destiny as planned by God, and that they will go to God through their life in the married state. The decree continues: 'For this reason, Christian spouses have a special sacrament by which they are fortified and receive a kind of consecration in the duties and dignity of their state' (*The Church in the Modern World*, §48).

For centuries, the Church has taught that marriage is a sacrament. Moreover, the theology of the Sacraments shows that marriage is one sacrament shared by both the spouses, and not two sacraments, one for each. It is a sacrament of unity for the couple, a sacrament which draws them closer to God. From this it is evident that there can only be one sacrament in a marriage; and there cannot be only a part of a sacrament—it is either there or not there. Then again, it is part of the Church's teaching that to be able to receive the other Sacraments it is necessary first to be baptized; it is necessary first to have been admitted into the Christian community. Consequently, it follows that for a couple to be able to receive the sacrament of matrimony, it is necessary that both the parties are baptized, are members of the Christian community.

From all this it will be seen that marriage will be a sacrament when both parties are baptized. Conversely, although the couple may be genuinely holy and receive enormous gifts from God, their marriage cannot be regarded publicly as a sacrament if both have not been baptized. On the other hand, if both parties are baptized into the Church even after their marriage has been celebrated, their existing marriage thereby becomes a sacrament. It should be stressed at this point that although a marriage may not be a sacrament, it is nonetheless assumed to be valid and binding. The couple who are parties to a non-sacramental union are nonetheless naturally bound to a permanent union.

However, the teaching of the Church maintains that where a marriage is not a sacrament, the Pope has power which he can exercise in very special circumstances to dissolve a non-sacramental union which has already broken down. This power of the Pope is often referred to as the *Petrine Privilege,* called such as an extension of the *Pauline Privilege.* This latter has as its authority Chapter 7 of the first letter of St Paul to the Corinthians (vv. 8-15). In this Epistle, St Paul warns the Corinthians (still living in a pagan world) that after becoming converted to Christ it might happen that the convert's married partner remains a pagan and refuses to live in peace without offence to the creator. In such circumstances, the Christian party was given permission to leave the pagan partner, so as to be able to lead a Christian life. Such a Christian was also given permission by St Paul to remarry, and it is the teaching of the Church that the first marriage is dissolved in the act of exchanging consent in the second union. The details of both the *Pauline* and *Petrine Privileges* will be studied in Chapter Eight. It is sufficient to note at this stage that where a marriage is not a sacrament, it lies within the power of the Holy Father to dissolve this union in certain special and restricted circumstances.

### III   CONSUMMATION

The Constitution *The Church in the Modern World* urges couples to nourish and develop their wedlock by conjugal love and undivided affection. It continues: 'This love is an eminently human one since it is directed from one person to another through an affection of the will. . . . This love the Lord has judged worthy of special gifts, the healing, perfecting and exalting gifts of grace and charity. Such love, merging the human with the divine, leads the spouses to a free and mutual gift of themselves, a gift proving itself by gentle affection and by deed. . . . This love is uniquely expressed and perfected through the marital act' (*The Church in the Modern World*, §49).

We have already mentioned the conflict which arose between the law schools of Paris and Bologna as to whether marriage was *made* by consent or by consummation. It was long held before this time that a sacramental marriage which had already been contracted was rendered indissoluble when it was consummated, since this act was a symbolic representation of the union between Christ and his Church. Conversely it was argued, that where a marriage had not yet been consummated, it was at least theoretically dissoluble because it did not yet bear the seal of the union of Christ with his Church. As in so many other matters, what appears to have determined the teaching of the Church was the actual practice of the Church. Although there were certain periods during the middle ages when some Popes did not allow dispensations to be granted in favour of remarriage when the original union had not been consummated, it was a slowly growing practice to allow this dispensation in certain closely defined circumstances.

It is indeed part of the teaching of the Church that if a sacramental and valid union has not been consummated, it is at least theoretically possible of dispensation. Some of the historical development of this practice and the rules relating to it, will be discussed later in Chaper Seven. At this stage, it is merely noted that the Church does grant such dispensations, and it is therefore part of the work of a tribunal, acting on behalf of the Holy See to assemble indications and proof that the marriage in question has not been consummated.

## IV   LACK OF FORM CASES

It has already been mentioned that Catholics are bound to the form of marriage unless there is some general or special dispensation granted for certain persons to be released from the law. Where a marriage takes place without such a dispensation, in a church of another denomination or in a register office, it is regarded as not being a union conforming to the rules of the Catholic Church. Sometimes it is the role of the marriage tribunal to deal with such cases. In most places, however, it is the task of the Chancery office of the diocese to deal with them. The invalidity of such marriages depends upon the rule that a 'baptized Catholic is bound to the *form of marriage*'. At present, there is much discussion about this law, and specially about whether it should be retained.

## V   ILLEGITIMACY

Many people are opposed to their case being presented to a marriage tribunal on the grounds that if the marriage is declared invalid, the children would automatically become illegitimate. In fact, this is not the case. The rule about illegitimacy is that where a child is born of a union that is known to be invalid by the partners at the outset—for example where two Catholics contract a marriage in a register office—the children are indeed regarded as illegitimate.

Illegitimacy is used here, of course, in the canonical sense, and has no relation to civil illegitimacy. There are only a few results of ecclesiastical illegitimacy: for example, it is a bar (without dispensation) to being raised to the episcopate.

However, when children are born to a union which is subsequently declared null and void on the grounds of some defect of consent on the part of one of the contractants, the children are regarded as being the offspring of a *putative* union. Such offspring are not regarded as illegitimate. Moreover, where there are children of a marriage which is dissolved on the grounds that the union is not a sacrament, there is no question of a putative marriage, since the basic presumption is that the marriage is valid. Hence, the question of illegitimacy arises in relatively few cases, and is not, practically speaking, of very much importance.

It has been the aim in this opening chapter to describe some of the fields in which the marriage tribunal works. The cases mentioned, involving nullity, dissolution or dispensation, will all be dealt with in subsequent chapters. It will already have been seen, however, that the scope of the tribunal is by no means confined to the nullity of marriage. Therefore, in the following chapters, in addition to an examination of the grounds for nullity and the formal judicial procedure, we will also deal with the non-consummation and the non-baptism cases, describing something of the historical background of each of these procedures, and covering the requirements of the modern-day process.

In speaking of the various processes which are the concern of the marriage tribunals around the world, it will be noticed that almost all of these procedures take a very considerable time, and an immense amount of care and attention is given to each individual case from the lowest tribunal to the Holy Father himself. The reason for this is obvious. A tribunal is dealing with a union which may be a sacrament, and may perhaps also be an indissoluble bond as established by Christ himself. For this reason, no tribunal can work with the speed or slickness of a civil divorce court, which is merely setting aside the civil effects of a union. A sacrament is something unique, requiring a process which will respect the dignity and essential holiness that is imparted to it by Christ; hence the care and attention to detail which must be given to the work. It is this factor which tempers the desire of every priest working in a tribunal to proceed speedily, and which shows the point of commencing the meeting of the judges for nullity decisions with the prayer to the Holy Ghost, and heading the eventual reasons (or *Sententia*) for the decision with the invocation of the Blessed Trinity.

# Chapter 2

# THE GROUNDS FOR NULLITY– CONSENT

A marriage can be declared null and void if there existed an undispensed diriment impediment at the time of the wedding. A marriage can also be declared null and void either if there was no consent given to the marriage, or if the consent was in some way defective. Each of the grounds will now be examined.

## I  TOTAL SIMULATION

There can be a situation in which a person, though he appears to give consent to his marriage, in fact does not give internal consent. It may appear strange that a person can go into such a solemn state as marriage with the 'intention of not contracting the bond' but this occasionally does happen. When consent is completely withheld, the union is null and void. The term given to this type of situation is *simulated consent,* or *total simulation.* For such a marriage to be proved null and void, the firm intention of not contracting the marriage, despite all external signs to the contrary, must be demonstrated by means of witnesses who knew about these facts before, during and after the wedding. Proof will be dealt with later on, but it is immediately evident that to demonstrate such total simulation can often be exceedingly difficult.

The law of the Code says clearly that the presumption must obviously be against such simulation, and very clear proof must be brought before a tribunal can rule that the marriage in question is invalid. Mere statements of the parties or opinions of the witnesses will not be sufficient—the simulation must be proved with real and irrefutable arguments drawn from the evidence of the case.

But there is a further general difficulty which arises in any nullity case. When a marriage has turned out badly, little by little a person—without any intention to lie or deceive—can come to think that he did not give consent at the outset, or that his consent was defective in some way. Innocent, though real, self-deception is always a problem; and this is one of the reasons why proof from external sources is required.

A person can, of course, allege his own lack of consent as a ground for nullity. He may have been in a situation of serious pressure—not sufficient for force and fear, but—sufficient to make him go through the external celebration of the marriage. The confusion and the pressure may have combined to remove all possibility of guilt; nonetheless until the facts have been made clear, the judges are bound to treat the allegations with great caution. However there may be persons who knew him at the time of the marriage and were aware that he was going to withhold all consent from the union. Such witnesses might be able to provide most useful evidence. Again, there may be documentary evidence that existed at the time of the marriage which shows that consent was going to be withheld from the marriage. Such evidence will also be most helpful. On the other hand, the judges would view with the gravest suspicion a document which was alleged to have been drawn up prior to the marriage; and which clearly sets out the person's intention to simulate his consent. Later we will deal with the acceptance or rejection of a petition from someone who is the malicious cause of the nullity; suffice it to say that the Church does not permit a person to profit from such malice, deception and injustice to the other party.

In spite of the fact that, by the nature of the case, proof of total simulation is difficult to find, such grounds are not impossible of proof. The jurisprudence of the marriage courts of the Church demands four basic requirements for such grounds to be ordinarily established. What these requirements amount to are 'indications of proof'. Firstly, it is necessary that there is some statement made by the person who simulated his consent. If the person concerned made a statement admitting the simulation just after the wedding ceremony, and there is a witness to testify to this, such evidence is extremely important. Secondly, there is required some reasonable explanation for the simulation. A reasonable explanation of the simulation might be the circumstances in which the person was browbeaten into marriage, or where strong pressure existed, or even grave fear. Thirdly, the jurisprudence of marriage tribunals demands that the circumstances surrounding the marriage point towards simulation as a possibility—for example, if a man deserted his wife directly after the wedding, and disappeared; or where he stated to other people after the ceremony that it had been a farce because he had not intended to marry. Finally, there is required—as in all cases—the evidence of persons other than the parties, who can support and confirm the statements and allegations made by the parties.

*First case on total simulation*

Henry was a young unmarried executive who had recently joined an important company; due to his good work, he had come to the

very welcome notice of the Chairman of the Board. An invitation to
the Chairman's home followed where Henry met the daughter,
Sonia. Initially he was attracted to her and she responded; but as he
got to know her better he found her to be spoilt, domineering and—
with other young men—flirty. Henry's position in the company
advanced and showed great promise. Sonia's mother took a hand
and decided that Henry would be a suitable match for Sonia. The
mother was even more domineering than the daughter; and she
began making plans for an engagement and wedding. Henry
meanwhile had met another girl, Belinda, much more to his liking
and these two fell in love. But try as he would he sensed that he was
becoming more and more committed to marry Sonia; not because of
any liking for her, but because of the mother; and specially because
the latter had subtly, but nonetheless clearly, indicated that unless
he did marry Sonia, his position in the company would be in
jeopardy. Not a strong character he felt trapped, and found himself
leading two lives. He did not dare tell Sonia about Belinda because
the mother would create havoc, he thought; and he did not dare tell
Belinda, whom he truly loved, lest this should spoil their
relationship. Very clearly he showed his own family that he was
deeply opposed to marriage with Sonia but felt he could not
endanger his career. He contrived with some ingenuity to see
Belinda right up to the day before the marriage; wrote to her three
times from his honeymoon hotel; and of course very soon the
marriage collapsed, and he went to live with Belinda. Not long
afterwards Sonia petitioned for a decree of nullity on the grounds of
Henry's total simulation, and on the basis of evidence from Henry
himself, Belinda, Henry's parents and Sonia's mother a decree of
nullity was issued.

*Second case on total simulation*

Peter and Mary were only seventeen when they first went out
with each other. Mary had been adopted and she had not had a
happy homelife with her adoptive parents. She and her adoptive
mother never got on too well; and Mary somewhat unjustly blamed
this unhappiness on the fact that this was not her own mother.
When the two youngsters had been going out for some while,
intercourse took place; but already Mary's interest in Peter was
waning. Shortly afterwards they parted. But then Mary discovered
that she was pregnant. She got in touch with Peter and they decided
to tell their parents. The two sets of parents were upset but
extremely kind and understanding. They felt that the two were
somewhat young and immature for marriage, but said that whatever
they decided they would stand by the youngsters; and if Mary

decided not to marry, the adoptive mother would help her with the baby. To everyone's surprise (knowing by now that Mary had tired of Peter's attentions), Mary announced that she was going to marry Peter. There did not seem to be any warmth or affection in this announcement; nor did she show any towards Peter. She merely insisted that she was going to marry him. With some anxiety the parents allowed the marriage to take place; and it turned out a disaster.

Mary did not want intercourse with Peter, though it did in fact take place a couple of times against her will. She made clear to Peter that now the marriage had taken place, he could do what he liked; as for her, she was going to remain with him until after the baby was born, and then return to her parents. Argue as he might Peter could not move her; and indeed after the birth of the baby she did return to her parents for a while and shortly afterwards left them to set up house on her own with the baby. Peter petitioned for a decree of nullity on the grounds of Mary's simulation. Good and convincing evidence was brought to show that Mary's whole mind had been to go through a ceremony of marriage with the father of the baby, so as to be able to produce a legitimate certificate of birth for the baby, but apart from that she was not interested in marriage or Peter at all. A decree of nullity was granted.

COMMENT ON THE TWO CASES OF TOTAL SIMULATION

It will be noted at once that there is a fundamental difference between these two cases. In the first case Henry did not want to marry Sonia, and if he had dared he would have run a mile from the situation. Thus equivalently when he was saying the words at the altar 'I do' and 'I will', his mind was stating the complete reverse, i.e. 'I don't' and 'I won't'. On the other hand in the second case Mary was adamant that she was going to get married; and no one was going to stop her; and yet that too is regarded as simulation. The jurisprudence of the Church has long perceived that a person may wish to go through a *form of marriage* and yet at the same time not want to enter into *the married state*. In Mary's case, the only way in which a document could be obtained to show that her baby was legitimate was by going through a form of marriage; and thereafter she showed no interest whatsoever in Peter. Thus the fundamental similarity, apart from these superficial differences, between the two cases is that neither Mary nor Henry intended to enter into the married state; to enter into what the Second Vatican Council termed the 'union of life and love'. Thus where it can be shown that the person in question has excluded this lifelong union, but has nonetheless gone through a ceremony of marriage, that is what constitutes the grounds of total simulation. In fact there are differing views, in terms of the Church's jurisprudence as to what the situation in Mary's case should be called; some would term this defective consent; others inadequate consent; others again lack of commitment. Whatever it may be termed, the situation still comes down to simulated consent.

### Renewal of consent

We have already made mention of the necessity for Catholics to be married before a priest and two witnesses (unless this obligation is dispensed for special reasons). If a Catholic does however go through a form of marriage in a register office or a church of another denomination without such a dispensation, then the resulting union is not regarded by the Church as valid. This is the law whilst the necessity of the *form of marriage* remains.

Subsequently should the Catholic party wish to set matters right, it would be necessary for his previous union to be rectified or *convalidated*. This involves the renewal of consent by both the parties—this time before a priest and two witnesses. It can, however, sometimes happen that the non-Catholic party may regard the existing union as valid; and to think of himself as married properly. He might regard the convalidation merely as a kind of blessing; but not as a marriage as such. If it can be shown that this was indeed how the non-Catholic looked upon the rectification, it can than be argued that therefore he did not renew his consent; and if he did not do this, then the convalidation itself was invalid. The minimum required for valid rectification of a previously invalid union is for the parties to accept that as far as the Church is concerned the previous union was null and void. But without this minimum acceptance then the invalidity of the convalidation can be alleged. It will be seen that this is merely one further application of the principle that marriage is made by consent; and without it there is no marriage—regardless of the words used.

### Condition and intention

We must now consider two further terms—namely *condition* and *intention*. It is possible for someone to marry with the intention of excluding from his consent some vital element which is involved in the contract of marriage. We have already said that true matrimonial consent involves permanence, fidelity and openness to children. If one of these elements, vital for the Christian contract of marriage, is excluded then the union would be null and void. An *intention* is a firm and positive act of the will whereby one of the essential elements involved in the Christian contract of marriage is excluded. An intention is not a mere thought about the possibility of some such exclusion; it is a firm and positive act of will expressed before the marriage.

On the other hand, a *condition* is a clause or stipulation which proposes that the essential obligations of marriage should either be qualified or nullified under certain given circumstances. For example, a person may make a condition that no consent is given to the marriage unless the couple live in the house of the bride's parents. Unless such a condition is properly fulfilled, the union would be null and void.

It will be seen, therefore, that although an intention *must* relate to some essential element of the marriage contract for there to be any possibility of invalidity, a condition *can* relate either to an essential element of the marriage, or to something entirely unconnected with marriage, such as where the couple are to live after the wedding. Practically speaking, the effect of an intention against some substantial property of Christian marriage, and the effect of a condition against one of these properties is the same. For this reason we will, in the following pages, discuss an intention against the substance of marriage and what is said there will also, practically speaking, relate to a condition made against the substance. On the other hand, we will deal separately with conditions which are not connected with the substance of marriage, such as mentioned in the example above.

When we described the ground of total simulation, it was shown that in such cases the consent required for a marriage was entirely lacking. In cases where an intention or a condition has been made against one of the essential properties of marriage, it could be said that there is *some* consent present, but it is *not sufficient*. It is in this sense that certain grounds come under the general heading of *partial simulation*. However, when discussing the grounds for nullity under this heading it is well to appreciate that if some essential element has been ruled out of the consent, then to all intents and purposes, there is not merely insufficient consent, but since consent is one and undivided, there is no consent at all to Christian marriage as such. Therefore, when a term such as *defective consent* is used, it is used in a less than strict sense. A person either gives consent which is whole and entire, ot he does not give proper consent at all. This is the reason why the marriage can be declared null and void. It is not the task of the judges to decide whether what consent was present was sufficient; they have to decide whether there was consent to Christian marriage or not. To say that a person's consent to a marriage was defective, therefore, is really the same as saying there was no consent to marriage, as understood in the Christian sense. Thus *total* and *partial* are merely ways of describing the consent, or lack of it, to Christian marriage.

One final point, before proceeding to examine the nature of defective consent, is connected with the use of the term *Christian marriage*. This is not primarily meant in the sense of marriage as *contracted by* Christians. What is meant here is marriage as understood by Christians. In a sense it is quite feasible for pagans to contract a Christian marriage if they have all the proper intentions which are involved in marriage as spoken of by Christ. The term Christian marriage is used to distinguish it from other unions in which, for example, the couple regard their union as dissoluble, since they have no idea of any other possible form of marriage. It is important to make this distinction between Christian marriage and other marriages, since in the present day there are many of the latter kind of unions contracted.

## II PARTIAL SIMULATION

In the previous chapter we examined marital consent in the light of the teaching of the Second Vatican Council. We pointed out three of the vital elements which constitute consent. The *Code of Canon Law* gives a short definition of consent, namely 'the act of will by which each party gives and accepts a perpetual and exclusive right over the body for acts which of themselves are suitable for the generation of children' (c. 1081, §2). The three basic elements involved here are the right to conjugal acts, a right which is perpetual, and a right which is exclusive. The exclusion of any or all of these three elements from a marriage contract means that the consent of the party concerned is defective, and the union would be null and void. We will now examine these three elements in the light of contrary intentions.

### THE INTENTION OF EXCLUDING THE RIGHT TO CONJUGAL ACTS

We can begin with the simple statement that if a person excludes from his consent the right of his partner to acts which 'of themselves are suitable for the generation of children', he would be entering into a union with defective consent, and the marriage would be null and void. To every human being there belong certain rights over the body—for example, a person has the right to decide whether he will have a leg amputated if the doctors advise this. This is the reason why a person has to sign a consent form before such an operation can take place. In the same way, each person possesses the rights over his body concerning the use of his sexual faculties. The Church teaches that these faculties may only be exercised within marriage. Moreover, for a valid marriage to take place, it is necessary that the parties exchange these rights over their bodies with each other, so that the rights which the husband once possessed over his own body are freely given over to the wife and those which the wife once possessed are freely given over to the husband. This exchange is a basic element in the marriage contract. If these rights to conjugal acts are not thus exchanged, the marriage is invalid.

What has been expressed above is stated in legal terms; and normally speaking, when two people marry, they do not give a thought to the exchange of these rights. Nonetheless, in another sense the couple know only too well that this exchange should take place. For example, after the marriage, they know something is wrong if it appears that these rights have not been exchanged. Thus if a woman discovers after the marriage that her husband refuses her the right to have children, she knows instinctively that there is something terribly wrong with the marriage. More than likely, this woman has no knowledge of Canon Law, but she does know there is something wrong. The law mentioned above from c.1081, §2, is merely the legal statement of these facts which every man and woman knows through their own nature, and through their own ordinary appreciation of what marriage means.

Having said that the exclusion of the right to conjugal acts would render the marriage null and void, we must now see what is meant more precisely by *the right to conjugal acts*. There are a number of different situations which are covered by this statement. One situation is where a man absolutely refuses his wife intercourse for some reason. Sometimes this appalling situation does arise, and after a few years the wife, broken in health and spirit, finally admits that her husband never once allowed her to have intercourse. Another situation is where one of the parties insists that intercourse should take place only within the safe period. Never once does he or she permit intercourse to take place at any other time. A third situation is when one of the parties insists upon making use of contraceptives whenever intercourse takes place, and this insistence upon contraceptives is quite clearly, and upon the person's own admission, so as to avoid all possibility of allowing the wife to have children. In each of these three situations— assuming that there is clear proof—the union would be invalid because one of the parties refused the right 'to acts which of themselves are suitable for the generation of children'.

We have been examining the situation as it has emerged through the investigation of the pattern of the marital life. What is vital in the examination of any marriage case is that the intention to exclude the right to proper conjugal acts is shown to exist at the *time of the wedding*. It is obvious that an intention formulated after the wedding has taken place would not mean that the right has been excluded from the contract of marriage. Only where the contract is mutilated by some exclusion from the consent at the time of the wedding would the union be invalid.

Bearing in mind that a person who enters a union with the clear, firm intention of not transferring to his partner the rights over his own body to conjugal acts would be entering the union with defective consent, it must also be said that a person entering marriage with the mere intention of abusing the rights to such acts *already conferred* would not contract invalidly. It is, at least theoretically, possible to think of the situation where a man freely and willingly grants to his wife the *right* to conjugal acts, but at the same time proposes for some of the time to abuse these rights by insisting on contraceptive intercourse, against her will. In these circumstances, because the right has not been excluded from the marital consent, the marriage would be regarded as, at least *prima facie,* valid. Thus, for example, if a newly married couple agree to make use of contraceptives until they are able to afford to start a family, they would not contract invalidly. Nor, in the situation where, contrary to the wife's wishes, the husband makes use of contraceptives *on some or even most occasions* of intercourse, would this marriage be invalid.

In these situations the judges in the case have to try to decide what the intentions of the person were when he entered marriage. As we will see later on, the burden of proof is upon the person alleging the invalidity, and it cannot be presumed that because of one of the parties insists on contraceptive intercourse he has therefore exluded the right to conjugal acts from his consent. This must be proved. To determine the precise intention of the parties existing at the time of the marriage is obviously extremely difficult. It is for this reason that often a large assembly of evidence must be collected.

It is also important to appreciate, when considering an intention to exclude the right to conjugal acts, that this intention must be a real one. An intention is a proposal formulated by the will, and not merely the knowledge of some situation in the intellect. For example, to say, 'I trust and hope we shall not have children' does not constitute an *intention,* since there is no specific act of the will formulated here. On the other hand, to say, 'I do not propose to have any children' is an indication of an act of will. As such, it would be described as an intention. There can be circumstances in which one of the parties may never have given thought before the marriage to the matter of children. Such a person might afterwards say: 'I did not make any act of will excluding children from the marriage, because I did not consider the matter. But if I had considered it, I would have excluded them'. Such a statement would merely mean that in certain circumstances an act of will would have been made, but the phrasing of the statement indicates that an act of will upon this vital matter was *in fact* not made. This type of intention *(I would have made it had I known)* is not sufficient to invalidate the marriage since it can scarcely be regarded as an intention as such.

There, can, however, be another kind of situation. For example, an engaged girl tells her fiancée before the wedding day that she does not propose to allow him to have children by her. Because of this the fiancée cancels the marriage. The girl appreciates that she should never have told her fiancée about her intention. Therefore, still with the same intention in mind, but now not even mentioned or adverted to in the second courtship, she marries someone else. Although she did not have the intention right in the forefront of her mind at the time of the marriage, nonetheless she had never rescinded the intention originaly made. In such circumstances, if proof is forthcoming of all the above, this type of intention would certainly suffice to render the marriage invalid.

*Case of exclusion of the right to conjugal acts*

Two graduate students, Michael and Olivia, married in a register office. Olivia was a Catholic. The couple intended to return to their home town and there celebrate the marriage in Olivia's parish church. This did in fact happen, though there was an interval of some ten days between the civil marriage and the wedding in the church. Even before the civil marriage, Olivia thought she sensed on the part of Michael an unwillingness to discuss the matter of children. But on the honeymoon, after the church wedding, Michael insisted on using contraceptives, in spite of his wife's protests. The excuse he made was that they could not afford children. However, as time went by, it became clear to Olivia that Michael was never going to have children by her, and not long before they parted he told her so in as many words. In fact it emerged that just before the time of the civil union Michael would have been prepared to have children, but after the civil ceremony, Michael happened to speak to some friends who told him that Catholics had to have children, and lots of them. He disliked this idea intensely, and before the wedding in church he made a clearly formulated intention not to have any children at all by Olivia. He made this intention quite clear to the friends he was speaking with, and hence, at the time of the ecclesiastical wedding, he already had an intention to exclude the right to proper conjugal acts with his wife. The case was decided in favour of the invalidity.

### THE INTENTION OF EXCLUDING THE INDISSOLUBILITY OF MARRIAGE

As we have already mentioned, one of the essential properties of marriage is its indissolubility. The consent given to the marriage is consent to a permanent and indissoluble union. It is considered that when a couple marry they intend to enter into the kind of marriage that God has instituted: that is, a permanent and indissoluble union. Although a couple may not even turn their minds to these essential properties of marriage, nonetheless it is assumed that this is their general intention. This, of course, is a presumption; and it is one that yields to contrary proof.

But it is possible for a person to enter into a union with the deliberate intention of terminating it in certain circumstances. In such a case, if the details could be established through the evidence, the union could be declared null and void. What is required is that the person concerned has a specific, clear and formulated intention to exclude the property of indissolubility from the marriage. Mere ignorance of the fact that marriage is permanent would not be sufficient. Here again, the deliberate act of the will in rejecting some clear essential element of marriage is required for the union to be invalid.

Unlike the previous ground we considered (the intention to exclude the right to conjugal acts) the present ground of the exclusion of indissolubility does not have the possibility of a distinction between the exclusion of an obligation and the non-fulfilment of the obligation. The permanence of marriage is either excluded or not. Once it is excluded, subject to proof, the marriage can be declared null and void.

From a practical point of view, this ground for nullity presents a number of problems. To illustrate one problem, if a man said to his fiancée that he did not necessarily intend the marriage to be permanent, there is a strong possibility that she would not marry him at all. More often, the man would not mention his intentions to his fiancée before the marriage. Hence, evidence would have to be found, if at all, amongst the man's friends to whom he may have communicated his premarital intentions. On the other hand, if both the parties had been of the same mind, namely that they did not wish their marriage to be permanent, this would constitute a ground for nullity if a petition were accepted for trial.

Another difficulty closely related to the one mentioned above is caused by the widespread practice of divorce in many western countries today. The prevalence of divorce makes possible the concept of impermanent marriage amongst people who have never had a religious upbringing, or perhaps never had any contact with a

Church since their purely formal Christening. For such persons, there is a chance that they would enter marriage quite ignorant of the fact that marriage is permanent and life-long. Up to now, Rotal jurisprudence has regarded this type of situation as mere *simple error*. The law of the Code states that simple error does not invalidate a marriage (*c.* 1084). Indeed, even when simple error is the cause of the marriage, it does not invalidate the union contracted.

However, the term *simple error* must be understood correctly. Where a person enters marriage and intends all those things which seem to be contained within marriage as he knows it, then the law of the Code applies, since this pattern of mind could be described as *simple error*. But there can be another situation—although this is not nearly so prevalent as the other mentioned above. A person may have been brought up in a religious atmosphere, but in his later years at school has rejected religion, religious values and, perhaps, even God. This person is able to contemplate the institution of marriage, and more or less make his own rules for this state. In such circumstances he is likely to reject the Christian values involved in marriage, and merely regard it as a stable relationship with some, but not an absolute, degree of permanence. Where this type of attitude is involved, it is possible that there may be grounds for nullity.

Nonetheless, for the general run of cases, it is required that a person excludes or rejects the essential permanence of marriage with a positive and formal act of will. In such circumstances the marriage would be invalid. It is important to follow the distinction between a formal exclusion and mere simple error. In the latter case, a person may *know* or *think* that marriage is not necessarily permanent, but until this knowledge has passed into the will there is no positive act of exclusion made by the will. On the other hand, the exclusion of permanence implies an act of will, and once this act of will is present then something integral has been rejected from the marriage contract. The consent given to the union in question is defective. Later, we will consider the situation in which the petitioner is the deliberate and malicious cause of the nullity through excluding the permanence of the marriage. It will then be seen whether such a person is allowed to petition before an ecclesiastical tribunal.

*Case of exclusion of the permanence of marriage*

Jennifer was baptised as a Catholic in infancy. She had a Catholic father and a non-Catholic mother. Her father rarely went to Church. Jennifer grew up in a not very religious atmosphere and ran wild as a teenage girl. She began going out with a young man, Edward, who was quite the reverse in character. He was also a Catholic, and under his influence, Jennifer started going to Mass again. However, she frequently grew impatient with Edward, probably resenting his kindly, stable and honest disposition. During this time she still had occasional flirtations with other young men, and one of these occasions involved her in intimacy. The girl became pregnant, and the boy responsible disappeared when he was told. Jennifer turned in desperation to Edward. He suggested that he should marry Jennifer: he said he loved her, and he would regard the child as his own. Jennifer refused at first, saying that she would rather have an abortion than marry, since a person could make such a terrible mistake by marrying the wrong person. But rather than tell her mother about the pregnancy, she agreed to marry Edward. However, she told several of her friends that this was a mere matter of convenience for her, since if Edward did not please her, she would leave him and find another man whom she liked better. Unfortunately, no one told Edward this, and though the marriage took place happily enough, it was not long after the birth of the baby that Jennifer began to find Edward's goodness a little too oppressive for her. She deserted him within a year of the marriage, leaving him with the baby.

Edward, after numerous attempts to persuade Jennifer to return to him, finally acknowledged defeat. Subsequently, he petitioned his local tribunal for a declaration of nullity on the grounds of Jennifer's defective intention concerning the permanence of marriage. After taking evidence of Edward and Jennifer, and from several of Jennifer's friends from before the marriage, the marriage was declared to be null and void, on the grounds of Jennifer's deliberate exclusion of the permanence of marriage. It will be noticed here that Jennifer's intention was a hypothetical one: that is, she did not say to herself before the marriage, 'I will leave Edward and go with another man'; she said, rather, 'If I don't find that I get on with Edward, I will leave him'. This hypothetical intention is sufficient to render the marriage invalid, since it also rejects the inherent indissolubilityof marriage from the contract.

THE INTENTION TO EXCLUDE FIDELITY FROM THE MARRIAGE

Parallel with the essential property of indissolubility or permanence in marriage, there is the equally essential property of fidelity. If either the unity or fidelity of the marriage is excluded by one of the parties, then the marriage is invalid. When a person contracts marriage he is presumed to include within his matrimonial consent all that marriage involves. Amongst other things, the couple are presumed to exclude as incompatible with a proper married relationship the possibility of marriage to a third party during the life-time of the two partners, or to exclude illicit relationships with other persons. However, though in the abstract it is possible to conceive of a situation where one of the partners to the marriage, for example, reserves to himself the inalienable right to keep a mistress during the married life of the other partner, this is somewhat unusual in everyday life.

The difficulty in this type of ground—the exclusion of marital fidelity—is the possibility of a distinction between the *right of fidelity conferred* or undertaken, and the *abuse of this right*. For example, it is possible to intend at the time of the marriage to be faithful to one's partner, and yet during the marriage to commit adultery. This is merely an example of the violation of an obligation. It does not indicate that the obligation of fidelity has not been undertaken. On the other hand, it is the clear and explicit rejection of the essential property of fidelity which is required to render a marriage invalid. Because the presumption in all marriage cases is for the validity of the union, it follows that where there is some indication of infidelity on the part of one of the spouses, these indications must be regarded as pointing towards the non-fulfilment of the obligation of fidelity, rather than towards the actual exclusion of the obligation. However, this presumption yields to contrary proof.

*Case of exclusion of the obligation of fidelity*

Frederick and Yvonne were married after a fairly lengthy courtship. Not long before the marriage, Frederick presented Yvonne with a document for both of them to sign. The document appeared to deal with property settlements, and amongst these details was a statement that Frederick intended to have complete freedom and liberty in 'everything'. Yvonne regarded this statement as somewhat cryptic, and she did not understand the full import of the statement until after the marriage. On the honeymoon, Frederick was reproved for his conduct with other women. At once, he declared that Yvonne had granted to him complete freedom in this and all other matters, in the document both had signed. From the very beginning of the marriage Frederick conducted himself as one who appeared to have no intention of binding himself by marriage. These facts were confirmed by other witnesses, and Frederick himself confirmed under oath that the meaning of the cryptic phrase in the document had been that he was reserving to himself the right to have intercourse with other women. All the evidence showed, moreover, that Frederick had conducted himself in this manner since the very beginning of the marriage. This was a clear case of the exclusion of the obligation of fidelity in marriage, and the petitioner, Yvonne, was granted a decree of nullity.

## III  CONDITIONS

We have already mentioned that there can be two general sorts of conditions: one that affects the rights to conjugal acts, or the permanence or fidelity of marriage, and the other sort that has no connection with these essential properties of marriage. We said that conditions which related to the essential properties of marriage were dealt with in the same way as intentions against these properties. Thus, in place of someone formulating the proposal: 'I intend to exclude the property of permanence from my marriage', he could also formulate the condition; 'I am marrying on the condition that I can terminate this union if the marriage breaks down'. Such a condition is dealt with in the same way as an intention. The same legal points are involved for both the intention and the condition when they regard some essential property of marriage.

There can, however, be other kinds of conditions which are not connected with these properties. The law about conditions is more complicated because of the number of types of conditions. To begin with, the Code states that three types of conditions are presumed not to have been seriously made. Again, this presumption yields to contrary proof. These three are future conditions which are either necessary, immoral or impossible. A *future necessary condition* is one which will be realised as a matter of necessity: for example, 'I will marry you if the sun rises tomorrow'. Such a condition is regarded as nonsensical, and it is reasonable to suppose it was not made seriously. A *future immoral condition* is one that would involve some base or immoral act; for example, 'I will marry you if you poison your mother'. Finally, there is the *future impossible condition* which makes the marriage consent depend on an impossibility. The law likewise pays no attention to this type of condition unless of course, clear proof removes the contrary presumption. Generally, therefore, the rule is that if a condition is immoral or impossible or necessary, it is regarded as having no effect whatsoever upon the marriage consent, saving clear proof to the contrary.

That, however, leaves another kind of condition which does not fall in the categories described above. This is the condition which is quite harmless and is certainly possible of fulfilment. If this type of condition is placed as a *sine qua non* to the marriage consent, the marriage consent is dependent upon the realisation of the condition

for it to come into existence. For example, a person could say that he
marries on the condition that all the children should be baptised and
brought up as Catholics. If this condition is not fulfilled then the
marriage is null and void.[1] However, if subsequently a condition is
alleged to have nullified the marriage it is important to establish that
it was placed as a *sine qua non* and not merely as an indication of what
one of the parties intends should happen in the marriage. A person
may intend that certain things should take place in the marriage,
such as the Catholic baptism and upbringing of the children. If the
marriage breaks down and in fact these intentions have not been
fulfilled by the other party, it is easy for the person who had the
original intentions about baptism and upbringing to come to the
state of mind where he *imagines* that he made a series of conditions
*sine qua non*. Such *afterthinking* is common in marriage tribunal
cases, and the judges have to be on guard for the situation when a
completely honest person petitions with the conviction that he
made certain conditions. On thorough examination, it often
emerges that the idea about conditions has become engrafted into
the person's mind since the breakdown of the marriage. As an
ordinary example, it is not unknown for two persons to give
independent and entirely different information about a car accident.
This discrepancy occurs in spite of the fact that both persons saw
the crash from the same point. The difference in the information is
usually the result of thinking, after the accident, about what *must*
have happened.

[1]   It will be appreciated that where such a condition is attached to the person's
      consent, this has the effect of suspending the marriage; i.e. the marriage does not
      legally come about until such time as the condition has been fulfilled. This is why
      the Church legislates against such conditions; and why the priest is instructed to
      discover whether the parties are entering marriage without conditions. In some
      circumstances the Bishop may forbid the marriage to take place until he is
      satisfied that all conditions have been revoked.

# Chapter 3

# THE GROUNDS FOR NULLITY—CONSENT
## (continued)

## I  CONSENT WHICH IS FORCED

We have been speaking above about consent given to a marriage, but which is in some way mutilated in that an essential property of the consent has been deliberately excluded. However, when we come to the ground of *force and fear* the situation is different. In spite of the fact that a person has entered into a union under threat or pressure, it is often still the case that the person concerned has given consent to the marriage. True, the consent has been forced, but consent is present. Consequently, this ground for nullity cannot be dealt with in the same way as the ground of total simulation. In fact, it is usually the exact reverse of that situation. In the case of total simulation it must be established that the person concerned gave no consent at all; in the case of force and fear, it is assumed that consent has been given. What has to be established is whether the force and fear was such as to remove the person's freedom in contracting the marriage.

It is obvious to the man in the street that if he was forced into marriage, then this choice was not a free act and there would be something wrong with the consent. This much is quite simple. The *Code of Canon Law* says that a marriage is invalid on the grounds of force and fear when such force and fear was unjustly caused by an external agent, to free himself from which the person was compelled to choose the escape offered by marriage (c. 1087). Of course, it is highly unlikely that a marriage could take place in circumstances in which a person is physically forced to go to the altar, for example, at gunpoint. But in spite of the unlikelihood of this situation, if it did occur the marriage would certainly be invalid. This much is quite clear. However, there are other circumstances in which the force is not physical, but rather moral compulsion. This is much more difficult because to all outward *appearances* the person concerned goes to the marriage quite freely, in spite of the fact that it is some form of moral compulsion that has really taken the person to the altar. Such moral compulsion or force, therefore, excercises upon the person concerned an influence which we speak of as fear. This is the reason why the grounds for this type of case are always stated as

'force and fear', since, for the fear to be produced, there has been
some form of force or moral compulsion used.

This makes it clear from the outset that the type of fear that is
needed to be a ground for nullity is that which is produced from
*outside,* or, as the Code says, produced by an external agent. Fear is
the 'disturbance of the mind caused by the apprehension of an
imminent or future danger', and the imminent or future danger
arises from the external agent responsible for the moral pressure. It
is necessary to state this, since a little thought shows that there can
be fears arising from all sorts of causes. If I am a hypochondriac, I
fear that I might have a heart attack. A girl might have all sorts of
fears on the day of her marriage. A man might fear that his shares
will depreciate and that he will lose a lot of money. All these are
examples of some sort of fear, but it is not this sort of fear that the
*Code of Canon Law* requires to invalidate a marriage. To help us
see the sort of fear that the Code has in mind, we must recall the
principle that if a person is not free to choose marriage, then the
marriage is invalid. Some fear removes freedom, and (apart from
psychological disorders) the kind of fear involved here is that which
is produced by some sort of external moral pressure. Hence, the fear
regarded by the Church as invalidating marriage will always be
related to some sort of pressure, physical or moral, from the outside.

Having said this, it will have been noticed that the Code insists
upon a series of conditions attaching to the fear so as to produce the
invalidity of marriage. First, the fear must be grave or serious: just a
passing dislike of a person, or merely firm but kindly parental
influence, would hardly cause fear serious enough to invalidate the
union. Next, the Code says that the fear should be unjustly caused;
then that it should be caused by an external source, and lastly that it
should be so compelling as to make the person concerned choose
marriage as the only means of freeing himself from the force or fear.
We will now deal with requirements, and also give a note about
what is often called reverential fear.

FEAR MUST BE GRAVE

There is a difficulty that immediately arises. How does one define
grave fear? What is serious or grave fear for one person might be a
mere light unsubstantial fear for another person. In the present
context, grave fear is examined as it would affect all men. This is
what might be called absolute grave fear. Fear is considered to be
*absolutely* grave if the 'evil that is threatened or feared is considered
by everyone as an absolutely grave harm', for example death or
mutilation, or serious loss of good name or infamy. On the other
hand, a much lesser degree of fear existing in someone else might

have, to all intents and purposes, exactly the same results as absolutely grave fear. This is often called *relatively* grave fear. This could arise as a result of some harm which would not be regarded as objectively grave by everyone, but *for this particular person*— because of the person's youth, or condition or disposition—it is regarded as a very serious evil or harm indeed. Where such relatively grave fear can be shown to have unduly interfered with a person's liberty of consent, the marriage must be regarded as invalid.

Obviously, the gravity of the fear and the condition, temperament or character of the person concerned must all be carefully studied. For example, a young girl who has led a very sheltered life, who has always lived at home and who has a soft and pliant disposition, would be far more vulnerable to moral pressure placed upon her by her parents than would a girl a few years older who has lived away from home in a flat for some time. Again, a girl would probably, though by no means always, be more prone to the effects of moral pressures than would a man.

One indication of the gravity of the fear is to see whether the person concerned took any steps, however ineffectual, to liberate herself from the moral pressure exerted. For example, a girl has been told that her grandparents are especially insistent upon her marrying a particular young man. Her parents are not insisting, and an appeal to them will be sure to remove the pressure upon the girl. However, if she went to stay with her grandparents who live isolated in the country, where she may expect to be subjected to serious pressure to marry the young man, then she can hardly be described as taking reasonable steps to free herself from the pressure exerted by her grandparents.

There is another form of fear which we have not yet mentioned. This is *reverential* fear. Obviously this is not, when objectively viewed, the same as *absolute* grave fear. Reverential fear would exist when one fears the indignation of a parent or superior or guardian, even though there may be no blows or threats. Clearly this type of fear is fairly slight. But if, in fact, it amounts—for this particular person—to *relatively* grave fear, and, coming from some external source, is unjustly caused, and leaves the person no liberty of choice but to marry, then it would indeed invalidate the marriage in question. This type of fear will become grave, depending upon the circumstances which surround it. Such circumstances would arise when there is constant nagging, endless harping on the subject, entreaties and similar indirect but nonetheless effective assaults on the person to such a degree that she is finally worn down and all resistance is overcome. On the other hand, the mere fear of offending a parent or guardian alone would not amount to *grave reverential fear*; nor, of course, would it be grave reverential fear if a girl married a man who was the preference of her parents, rather than her own preference, provided always that the actual choice she did make was not against her will.

### FEAR CAUSED BY AN EXTERNAL AGENT

We have already shown that for fear to invalidate a marriage it must be at least comparable to the situation of a person who is physically forced into marriage. It follows, as we have demonstrated that the pressure or force which causes the fear must be caused by an *external* agent. It would not normally be sufficient for a person to have some internal fear or anxiety which convinces him that the proper course to adopt is this marriage. The external source can be another person or a group of persons, but the source must be a free agent. For example, though a tremendous storm might cause fear and terror in a person—such fear is obviously caused from an external source—this would not be sufficient to invalidate the marriage because it could not be regarded as moral pressure exercised by an external free agent. Thus, *normally,* fear of the loss of reputation, imaginary fears of misfortune, fear of disease, fear of eternal punishment—all these are fears which are produced in the mind of the person, and not by an external free agent. Moreover, the fear must relate to harm that will befall the person himself. For example, if a girl threatens to commit suicide if the man will not marry her, this could not *normally* be regarded as an evil which threatens the man himself. The evil, in fact, threatens the girl with the gun pointing at her head. Internal fear of this sort does not, *in ordinary circumstances,* violate a person's own liberty of choice. However, the precise circumstances will always be carefully investigated by the court to see if they do amount to grave fear.

All that has been said about fear being produced by an external free agent in no way prejudices the possibility of someone alleging that obsessional or psychological fears induced him to marry. This, however, is a point which must be dealt with when the ground of insanity and similar mental afflictions is considered later.

### FEAR UNJUSTLY CAUSED

It may seem unnecessary to mention this point, since there is a sense in which any fear that is caused, being sufficient to make a person contract marriage to escape the effects of the fear, would be unjust. Needless to say that, where force or fear are imposed on a child by its parents sufficient for it to have to contract marriage to escape these effects, this would be unjust fear. For example, a boy might become engaged to a girl and she then decides for entirely frivolous reasons not to marry him. A parent would be justified in pointing out with some asperity that the reasons given by the girl for the wreckage of the marriage plans are entirely unsubstantial, and that she ought to reconsider her decision. However, the parent would not be justified in going so far as to threaten, cajole, or nag the girl into marriage, if her mind is made up against the union. It will be seen, therefore, that the matter of injustice must be looked at both from the point of view of the person threatened, and from that of the person threatening.

There is another point here. An interesting case has arisen where the law of the country has a sanction against a man making a girl pregnant. It can occur that civil law (as has occurred in the U.S.A.) may prosecute a man for making a girl pregnant. Often the statutory penalty is imprisonment or a fine. It would be entirely unjust for a judge to impose marriage as a penalty. Or, in the case where the law permitted the option of marriage or a fine, it would be unjust of the judge to allow only the alternative of marriage, when the person concerned is willing to pay the fine. However, it would of course be argued today (and in our opinion, rightly) that no state has the power to impose marriage as a penalty for some act, even, for instance, rape or seduction.

MARRIAGE AS THE ONLY COURSE ALLOWED

The law states that the force or fear must be imposed so that marriage is the only way by which the person can free himself from the force or fear. What this means is that if a person with two *possible* courses open to him—one being marriage, the other escape to South America—chooses marriage and not South America, he would not be faced with marriage as the only course. The point being that marriage must be inescapable once the moral pressure and the fear have taken effect. This much is obvious.

However, it will be seen that, so far, we have been considering the situation where marriage is presented as one of the alternatives or as the only possible course. But the situation can arise when marriage is not presented as an alternative at all. For example, a young girl is being forced by her parents to enter a convent, which the girl does not want to do. Her parents threaten her, scold her, and try every kind of trickery to induce her to enter. The girl knows that if she stays at home much longer her parents will get the better of her and she will have to enter the convent. It is not possible, due to her circumstances, for her to leave home alone. She, therefore, tells them she will marry a certain young man, the only one she knows and whom she despises; but thinks marriage would be less odious than entry into a convent. Her parents agree to relent if she does marry the young man. This situation could be construed as presenting the girl with no alternative but marriage to escape her predicament, even though marriage was not one of the alternatives offered her originally by her parents. If it can be shown to be her only escape, the marriage could be declared invalid.

*Case of nullity on the grounds of force and fear*

Jack was eighteen and Cynthia was seventeen when the couple met. Neither were religious people, and after a comparatively brief association the couple began having intimate relations on almost every occasion they met. Not long afterwards Cynthia became pregnant. The girl tried several methods of inducing an abortion, but all without success. Eventually Cynthia told Jack that he would have to marry her. At first Jack refused, and so Cynthia's mother told the boy's mother of the pregnancy. The boy's mother insisted that Jack should marry the girl, and this insistence was repeated with constant nagging and anger, together with the threat of turning Jack out of doors if he would not go through with the marriage. Eventually Jack gave in to this coercion, but even at the last moment he tried to escape by going away with some friends on the night before the marriage. His mother discovered the plan and forbade him to leave the house, and again he capitulated. On the day of the marriage in the register office, he brought himself to a state verging on intoxication. The marriage broke down soon afterwards. The marriage was judged to be invalid on the grounds of force and fear.

It is important to appreciate that the fear which drove Jack to capitulate to his mother's wish is not construed as *terror*. Fear is a much lesser state than this, and it would not be proper for a court to demand as much as this to prove the alleged grounds. Fear is a state of mental trepidation, but it does not go as far as sheer terror, although the state of sheer terror would, of course, be a basis for a declaration of nullity. It will also be noticed from the above true case that the subject of the force was a man. Although from the nature of things it is more frequent that a girl should be the subject of force on the part of her parents or guardian, the situation can also arise with a man. However, though such cases—involving both men and women as petitioners—are not unusual these days, they are not frequent. There is a marked drop in this type of case, which was much more common forty years ago or more.

## II   IGNORANCE OF THE NATURE OF MARRIAGE

To state that a person must not be ignorant of the nature and obligations of marriage, so as to contract validly, seems like stressing the obvious. In the present day it would seem that a claim of ignorance could hardly arise. However, there are places where such ignorance is not uncommon; hence, this ground is mentioned here. The degree of knowledge required for marriage appears to be fairly minimal. As long as the parties contracting the marriage are aware of the fact that their marriage is to be a permanent union for the begetting of children through some sort of physical co-operation, the marriage is valid, even though the couple may have no very precise knowledge of the physiological facts of human generation. Even a vague idea would suffice for validity.

The Code states that after the age of puberty, such ignorance about marriage is not presumed, and must be proved. Puberty for a girl is regarded as being reached at the age of twelve, and for a boy at the age of fourteen. Since, however, most civil laws require a much higher age for marriage, it means that whenever anyone marries he is certainly presumed to know at least the basic minimum required.

The jurisprudence of local courts and the Rota shows that it is a matter of extreme difficulty to establish such ignorance. We have already dealt with the situation of *simple error*, so this point need not be repeated here. Normally, when the ground of ignorance of the nature and obligations of marriage is alleged, it is usually the facts of life which are implied. More often than not in such cases, there appears to be some positive evidence that the marriage in question has never been consummated. For this reason, there is a special provision in the rules governing nullity processes that such cases can be changed from the allegation of nullity to a plea for the dispensation of the marriage on the grounds of non-consummation. The latter type of case will be dealt with later.

*Case of nullity on the grounds of ignorance.*

Rosella was a young innocent girl of eighteen when she met a sailor named Malcolm. She had had a very protected upbringing; the facts of life had never so much as been mentioned in her home. Courtship with Malcolm involved the constant presence of a chaperone. Prior to the marriage her mother did get as far as mentioning that within the confines of the bedroom, Malcolm might "do things to her which were somewhat personal" but that she should not mind this, because "that's what men do". Completely mystified, Rosella went thus into marriage and her honeymoon. She appreciated after the first night what her mother must have been talking about; but she accepted in good part the intimacy which did take place. She was extremely keen on having a family. But as far as she was concerned children would come about through her sleeping between sheets which Malcolm had slept between. He was a sailor and spent regular fortnightly spells at sea; and on such occasions, Rosella might solemnly take out the sheets used previously by Malcolm and sleep between them in the hope of conceiving a child. The connection between physical intercourse and having a child never occurred to Rosella. In due time she began to complain of the physical intimacy to which she felt she was subjected by her husband, and not long afterwards returned to her mother. Malcolm alleged Rosella's ignorance as a ground for nullity and when these facts were established and proved, a decree of nullity was granted.

### III(a)   ERROR OF PERSON

The term *error* in Canon Law has a very precise meaning, but this is only what one would expect, since there are any number of uses to which we put the word in ordinary conversation. There can be an error in the accounts, an error in spelling. We speak of someone repenting of the error of his ways, and so on. Error is defined in Canon Law as the false judgement of an object. Quite clearly it is something very different from ignorance. Ignorance is the mere lack of knowledge, whereas error is a positive judgement which is mistaken. Ignorance exists solely in the intellect, whereas error implies a mistake involved with the function of the will. There are two forms of error, practically speaking, with which the *Code of Canon Law,* in connection with marriage, is concerned. One is 'error of person', in which a man marries the wrong person. The other is an error of, or about, the quality of a person but which in itself amounts to an error of the person.

Error of person is quite straightforward. Where a person alleges this type of ground of nullity, also called substantial error, he is actually alleging that the person he intended to marry was not the person he did in fact marry. This could only happen, clearly, as a result of substitution of one person for another. There have been such cases presented before local courts and the Rota, and they make incredible reading. But since in the current law of the Church, proxy marriages are still allowed, such cases can arise even today.

*Case of nullity on the bāsis of error of person*

Sandro and Catherina met in the south of Italy when they were twenty-four and twenty-two years old respectively. A friendship grew up between them, and after a year or so they thought they would like to get married. However, Sandro did not have a good job, and they both thought that he might improve himself if he went to England and worked on a fruit farm there. Thus Sandro went to England and began work, and after a further year he had saved a substantial sum of money and could certainly afford to marry and keep his wife. In the meantime, Catherina had met another young man, Pietro, who had much better financial prospects than Sandro. Little by little, she realized that she would be happier with Pietro than she would with her fiancé. She told her parents about her problem, and at first they thought she should marry Sandro, but they, too, were converted by the realization that Pietro had better employment and a much better future.

Meanwhile, Sandro was making arrangements to marry, but being in England he found that he could not get permission for Catherina to enter the country unless they were already married. Therefore, he made use of the device in Canon Law known as the proxy marriage. By this, he found he had to appoint someone in his home town in Italy to represent him at the marriage ceremony to be celebrated there. He was advised that this representative would make the promises at the altar together with Catherina, at the end of which Sandro would be regarded as married to Catherina. Sandro appointed his future brother-in-law, Giuseppe, as his proxy, and the necessary documents were signed to this effect. The local priest was approached by Catherina's parents with the necessary papers, and he agreed to celebrate the marriage on a particular Saturday.

When the day of the wedding came, Catherina was adamant that she would not marry Sandro. But, in the meantime, her parents had had a serious dispute with Sandro's parents. Hence, Catherina's mother and father refused to go to the Church. Taking this opportunity, Catherina sent her sister Maria to the Church, and throughout the ceremony Maria made the responses together with Sandro's proxy, Giuseppe. After the wedding ceremony, nobody noticed anything strange about the young bride keeping her veil down over her face, and Maria even signed the register in her own name without anyone noticing.

Following the ceremony, Sandro was expecting his wife to come to England, but she did not arrive on the date arranged. He made enquiries in Italy and found that Catherina had indeed left the country, but had gone to Argentina with Pietro. When enquiries were made into the matter, it was discovered that the person who had actually taken part in the marriage ceremony was Maria and not Catherina. Therefore the marriage was declared null and void on the grounds of 'error of person'. It is clear that, normally, it is only in the case of proxy marriage that such a mix-up could occur so as to amount to the invalidity of the marriage.

## III(b)   ERROR OF QUALITY

The Code states that an error concerning a quality of a person does not invalidate the union unless the error about this quality can be considered to amount to an error about the person. A mere error about a quality a person possesses might be seen in the situation of a girl thinking that her husband-to-be was a kindly person who would have no objection to her spending a lot of time with her girl friends. She discovers after the marriage that he does not approve of this. She was in error about her husband's character in this respect; but this would not be regarded as sufficient to invalidate the marriage.

On the other hand, there are certain kinds of quality which a person may possess that are of such significance as to specify or differentiate that person; and the lack of such qualities—because they are so significant—might make him (equivalently) an entirely different person. This is the area of an error of quality which amounts to an error of person. In the older text books the examples given of what is meant here by the law were drawn from an entirely dynastic concept of marriage. For instance, it was stated, a girl might accept a young man's proposal of marriage thinking (wrongly) that he was the Prince of Wales; that is the first son of the Monarch and the heir to the throne. However if he turned out to be the second son, then he would not be heir to the throne. The older text books would have regarded the possession of the quality of "being the Prince of Wales" as of such substance as to make the young man she actually married (the second son) a totally different person.

However more recently there have been developments in the Church's jurisprudence, which have been allied to the changing concept of marriage; that is marriage now seen not in specifically dynastic terms, but in terms of a personal relationship between two people. Thus it would be true to say that a person is specified *as this particular person* as a result of his own personal history and background. Where there is an error concerning the whole of this, then it might be said that such an error (of quality) may amount to an error of person. For example, where a girl entered into marriage with a man who turned out eventually to have been civilly married previously (though canonically free) with children by his first union, then she could claim that these facts pointed to him as being a different person to the one she thought she had married. She thought she had married a man who was single, who had no ties and no previous quasi-matrimonial relationship. It is true that the girl would not have specifically made all these as conditions to her marriage; but she would certainly have taken as given data these ordinary, fundamental requirements. The fact that he was not free of all ties, had been married before, certainly would make him a different man to the one she thought she had married. Where the quality of the person (concerning which there is error) is so significant and substantial as to make him a different person without such a quality, then there would be grounds for a nullity petition.

*Case of nullity on the grounds of error of quality*

Pierre, a Catholic, aged thirty-five entered a civil marriage from which union two children were born. Within a few years he had abandoned his family. During the second world war he had assisted the Germans in France, and afterwards he had been tried in his absence for being a traitor and was sentenced to twenty years' imprisonment. However he had disappeared, and escaped the law. Then he turned up again now aged 58, posing as a single person, as the nephew of a highly placed government official, as a doctor of medicine and a member of an important university faculty. He married Colette who found all the various qualities and his assumed background to be very suitable. The marriage collapsed within weeks because of Pierre's arrest by the police for his crimes during the war, for posing as a doctor and for pederasty. Colette petitioned for a decree of nullity and it was granted on the basis that Colette's consent in going through the form of marriage with Pierre had been directed towards a man known as single, a doctor and of good repute—all of which Pierre was not.[1]

---

[1]   It will be appreciated that in this case there might well have been a jurisprudential argument as to whether the grounds should have been (as here) error of quality amounting to an error of person; or perhaps an implicit condition on the part of the girl, to the effect that she intended to marry a man who was free, of good repute etc. The fact that this condition was not fulfilled might be regarded as having invalidated the union. In addition—in the proposed new Code—there would be a ground of nullity here on the basis of fraud (or *dolus*).

# Chapter 4

# AMENTIA, LACK OF DUE DISCRETION AND INABILITY TO FULFIL THE OBLIGATIONS OF MARRIAGE

The field of mental disorder may be regarded as the most complicated area of nullity grounds. One obvious reason is that it is one where the assistance of other sciences, and specially the psychiatric sciences is vital; and psychiatry is a study which is itself fast developing. Added to this, there is always the practical difficulty involved in these cases because evidence may be difficult to find. Information concerning a person's mental state is often deliberately hidden by relatives; the latter frequently refuse to cooperate—for understandable reasons; and how precisely to evaluate medical reports when they are available—all of these elements make for serious difficulty. We propose here to deal first with *amentia*, which is frequently but wrongly translated as insanity. Wrongly translated because though insanity is a form of *amentia*, the latter is far wider than insanity and covers many more conditions. Secondly, we will deal with the ground of nullity referred to as the lack of due discretion, which does not involve *amentia*; and thirdly, we will cover what is termed the inability to fulfil the obligations of marriage.

## I  AMENTIA

This is a latin term which refers to a person not being in a position (for reasons we will see in a moment) to bring his whole mind to a decision, to making the act of consent. For example, a person who is asleep cannot bring his mind to make an act of consent. Nor can a person who is completely drunk; or under the influence of some form of drug. A person on an LSD 'trip' would be regarded as being *amens*, as would someone under the influence of heroin; likewise when a person is under anaesthesia or hypnosis. Where a person does not enjoy the full advertence of his mind, this is regarded as being a form of *amentia*; and in this condition a person is not regarded as being able to make an act of consent (or at least make it properly); and consequently marriage which takes place in such circumstances is regarded as being null and void.

*Amentia* also covers the far more serious and destructive conditions such as schizophrenia, in its various forms; paranoia; manic depression; general paralysis of the insane and other serious mental disorders.

The basic question that faces the judges here is whether the person concerned had the ability to consent, or whether the condition from which he suffered removed his ability to make an act of consent—that is to say, whether the person was able to exercise freely, his will to consent to the marriage in question.

All that we can do here is to state some of the principles to which ecclesiastical judges have to conform when they are considering such cases. Once insanity has been established as having existed both before and after the marriage, it may be presumed that the same state of insanity existed at the time of the marriage. There is a presumption *against* the existence of lucid intervals at the time of the wedding. The point here is that although it is possible that a person may have been insane before the marriage, and shown to have been insane after the marriage, it is theoretically possible that he may have recovered sufficiently at the time of the marriage to give consent. But since this possibility is so remote, and on occasion would seem to run directly contrary to the best established psychological opinion, the law presumes that lucid intervals do not occur, at least not such as to render the consent sufficient. Medical science has demonstrated that when a person is insane there can be, at some stage, a *remission* or disappearance of the symptoms of the illness. However, it is maintained that this does not mean that the disease itself has disappeared, merely that the symptoms have been submerged for the time being. Hence it would obviously be wrong to assume that a lucid interval did occur. Indeed, even if a lucid interval had occurred, it would be extremely doubtful that the consent would have been any more effective during the period of remission than during the time of the clearest manifestation of the symptoms.

On the other hand, it is also drawn from canonical jurisprudence that mental derangement appearing after the marriage does not necessarily mean that the same illness in fact existed before the marriage. This must be proved. It will also be appreciated that mere committal to a mental institution does not carry with it the presumption that the person is unable to consent. There are, of course, very strict laws about the procedure for committal of persons to mental institutions but nonetheless such committal or voluntary hospitalization does not automatically mean that a person was unable to consent to marriage.

Again, judges have to be guided by the opinions provided by

psychiatric experts. But a note of caution here is sounded by the
Rotal Jurisprudence. It is stated quite clearly that the decision as to
the invalidity of the marriage rests with the judges and not with the
medical experts. Though careful attention must be paid to the
expert opinion, nonetheless because a doctor is not an ecclesiastical
judge; it is not his role to decide on the case as such. Then again, it is
important that the statements of the witnesses should be considered
most carefully. For example, when considering the evidence of the
ordinary witnesses, a careful distinction must be drawn between the
routine or habitual actions of the person concerned—such as
require little or no mental exertion—and the other actions which
demand a sane and deliberate act of the will.

In general however two things may be said in connection with the
grounds of *amentia*. Firstly, the actual consideration and evaluation
of evidence about such a condition is principally determined by the
constant practice of the courts, both local and Rotal. This constant
practice, or jurisprudence, must take into account the best
information available from the medical and psychiatric sciences, as
well as the application of such information to the basic principle,
that consent makes the marriage. Where it can established that due
to whatever condition, the person in question was unable to bring a
sound and whole mind to the act of consent, then the marriage
would be regarded as null and void. The second, and final, point to
be made here is that if it is the case that a person can show that there
was a mental condition pre-existing the marriage, and this
condition reappeared after the marriage, then it is always worth
while approaching a diocesan tribunal for the consideration of the
facts by Canon Lawyers. For obvious reasons it is not necessary to
give a case illustrating the grounds of *amentia*.

## II   THE LACK OF DUE DISCRETION

This is an area of the Church's jurisprudence which is specially
delicate and not a little complicated. The concept itself goes back
many centuries; and can even be found in the work of the work of
the disciples of St Thomas Aquinas. To put it briefly the notion of
due discretion refers to a certain judgemental ability concerning the
act of (and the obligations attached to) marriage. It may help to give
a few examples to convey the point. A young boy of twelve is left a
legacy of a million pounds. Although the money is indeed his, the
law of the land does not permit him to administer his fortune. The
boy knows he owns the money; he may even know how to write a
cheque; he knows that a million pounds is a lot of money. But the
law does not regard him as being capable of the necessary informed
decisions which would be required to administer the legacy.

In the same way, a girl of thirteen, well instructed in her convent school can know that marriage involves permanence, fidelity, openness to children. But she would not be regarded as capable of making the necessary judgements concerning what all these elements (and the many others) involve. She may perhaps be physically mature; she may even be capable of conceiving and giving birth to a child. But still she would not be regarded (at least in ordinary circumstances) as marriageable.

The point of both these examples is that there is a difference between knowing something, on the one hand; and being able to *evaluate* that same thing, on the other hand. To know some fact is quite different from appreciating the implications of that fact. This ability to appreciate the implications of marriage comes evidently with experience and a degree of emotional and psychological maturity. But without this required degree of maturity, the person is as yet quite unable to make informed or critical decisions; and as such the Church does not regard such a person as being able *at that stage* to enter into marriage.

One of the (many) problems which will immediately be perceived here is that this is an extremely grey area. Some cases of the lack of due discretion are very clear and straightforward. The lack of the ability to evaluate or assess the obligations to be undertaken in marriage is quite evident. However more often it is extremely difficult for the judges to weigh up the situation accurately.

One of the ways in which the situation may become clearer for the judges is to scrutinise very carefully the cause of the alleged lack of due discretion. It might be caused simply and solely by sheer immaturity (as in the cases mentioned above). The evidence for this may well show the true situation prior to the marriage; as well as the behavioural pattern afterwards—all of which may point very clearly to the lack of this required evaluative ability i.e. to the lack of due discretion.

In the situation considered above, the cause of the lack of due discretion was immaturity—emotional and psychological. It cannot be said that there is here any (necessarily) serious psychiatric condition or problem; just a sheer lack of maturity. However in other cases a person may already be in his middle or late twenties; and yet still be seriously immature. In such a case, the judges may be assisted by psychiatry.

One of the areas of great development made in psychiatry is in the field of what is called the personality disorder. This is not insanity; does not involve a psychosis; the person in question knows exactly what he is doing. But at the same time he suffers from a very severe case of what is considered to be constitutional immaturity; i.e. one which the years will not alter, as least for the better. Sometimes evidence in a case will show that the person was so crippled by the personality disorder that he was quite unable to evaluate or assess what is involved in the obligations to be undertaken in marriage. Thus here the lack of due discretion is caused by an identifiable psychiatric condition; and if the condition is serious enough, then the union entered by this person would be regarded as null and void.

The kind of psychiatric condition which might produce such a lack of due discretion would extend to the condition of a psychopath (in the clinical rather than the criminal sense); to an hysterical personality disorder; alcoholism of some great severity; male and (less often) female homosexuality; obsessional states; depression etc. It must be appreciated that the psychiatric tag given to some condition is not, and never can be, the 'ground for nullity' as such. One of the grounds of nullity here might be the lack of due discretion which is caused by a psychiatric condition. This reservation is important because what is being alleged in a case of the lack of due discretion is the lack of an informed act of consent; not a psychiatric state. Moreover it is the judges in the case who give the decision, and not the psychiatrist as noted above. The decision of the judges turns on their consideration of the person's discretionary ability or judgemental capacity, and not specifically upon whether the person is an hysteric or a psychopath.

It is also worth pointing out here that this ability to make the necessary critical judgement or evaluation refers specifically to the obligations involved in *marriage*. This is mentioned because it is well known to ecclesiastical judges as well as to psychiatrists that a person can have superb judgement and shrewdness in connection with his business ventures, and yet have no such ability or evaluative capacity with regard to his marriage. Stockbrokers, members of parliament, lawyers and doctors may be brilliant in their field; and yet still lack due discretion. Experience has shown that this is something which cuts right across all barriers of class, profession, colour and social scale. However, difficult though it is, the final decision (as in the case of *amentia* and the inability to assume the obligations of marriage to which we shall turn next) must be taken by the judges in the light of the Church's jurisprudence. which like everything else is a developing science.

*Case of nullity on the grounds of the lack of due discretion (severe immaturity).*

Patrick was just seventeen when he met Paula; she was nearly sixteen. Both were fairly wild; they had left school at fifteen. He had lazed around, not much helped by his own family background; and he had already been in trouble with the police for some wild prank. Paula worked but she regarded her wages as entirely intended to allow her to keep up with the fashion in dress. The couple began going out with each other in a desultory fashion, just as they did with other partners as well. The only special characteristic of their association with each other and with other partners was having intercourse everytime they met. Paula, not surprisingly, became pregnant; and she was with reasonable accuracy able to determine that Patrick was the father. She in no way took fright at the pregnancy; indeed she regarded it as a novel experience, finding herself at the centre of her friends' attention. Patrick acted as if nothing had happened. Only after some months did someone suggest to Paula that it might be an idea to get married; and she thought this was a good idea. Patrick said he thought it would be fun; and so with parental permission they married, he aged seventeen and five months; she aged sixteen and three months; and five months' pregnant. Neither had any money saved; but her mother gave them a room in her house. Some days after the marriage Patrick decided to get a job and earn some money. Paula continued her work in a hairdressing establishment. Neither of them paid anything to her mother for their keep; and both continued behaving as they had before the marriage. When Patrick began to earn some money he spent much of it on drink and betting. He also continued seeing other girls after the marriage as he had done right up to the time of the wedding.

When Paula went into hospital to have the baby, Patrick managed to visit her there once, though he was not on hand to take her to the hospital. When she came out with the baby, Patrick was much taken with the new experience of being a father; but this did not last for long; and he returned to his friends, to drink and the betting shop. However by this time Paula began to take her responsibilities as a mother rather more seriously. When eventually she remonstrated with Patrick for not helping with the baby nor bringing home any money (since she herself was not working), he was quite unable to see any reason at all for changing his ways. Finally Paula's mother, thinking that the only thing to bring Patrick to his senses was to give him a jolt, put both of them and the baby out of the room. Paula—not Patrick—set to, to find alternative accommodation. When she found some rooms Patrick promised to 'do them up', but he never got round to it. Patrick produced money for a few weeks for rent and food, but then stopped. When Paula started to nag him to pull up his socks, he told her he was bored with her, and left her; and went to live in his parents' home. That was the last she saw of him.

Sometime later Paula obtained a divorce with a view to trying to ensure maintenance from Patrick, but even that was sporadic. She then met a Catholic, and as a result petitioned for a decree of nullity so as to marry him. The grounds alleged were the lack of due discretion; and evidence of Patrick's crass immaturity was brought forward in abundance to prove the grounds; and a decree of nullity was granted.

## III   THE INABILITY TO ASSUME THE OBLIGATIONS OF MARRIAGE

This is a ground for nullity which in some respects is simpler for the judges of any tribunal to assess. The chief reason for this concerns the nature of the proof which is required to establish the grounds. This proof very much relates to the behavioural pattern of the person in question during the period after the marriage (as much as before it).

The principle upon which this ground is based is that 'no one is bound to the impossible'. The idea is that there are some persons who cannot undertake to assume the responsibilities and obligations of marriage; and as such cannot be regarded as marrying validly. To take a practical example from the jurisprudence of the Church's courts: a girl was diagnosed with certainty as a nymphomaniac. She met a young man with whom she fell in love. She also thought as a result of this new experience that her condition was cured. She told her psychiatrist who did not agree with her. He warned her that what she took to be a cure was merely a remission of her symptoms. She paid no attention to this advice and married. Within three months the condition had reasserted itself (i.e. the symptoms returned), and the marriage broke down. She was totally unable to be faithful to her husband. It will be seen that this girl was incapable of fidelity; i.e. one of the fundamental obligations of marriage; and consequently she was incapable of marriage itself.

The obligations that are involved here, initially, are those arising from the qualities of permanence, fidelity and openness to children. But, as we have already noted in Chapter One, the Church teaches that marriage is not only a contract (with its attendant rights and corresponding obligations); but it is also a relationship between two persons. It is the closest, most intimate of all possible relationships. Therefore for two persons to 'leave mother and father and cleave together in one flesh' requires an ability to form and sustain this close interpersonal relationship.

It must be noted here that when we are speaking of the inability of someone to form this close interpersonal relationship, we are not just speaking of an unhappy marriage of a couple who just 'didn't get on'. It cannot be said that a marriage which is unhappy is null and void. What the judges are looking for in such a case is the proved inability to form and sustain a recognisable marital relationship. The cause of this inability is often some serious psychosexual or psychiatric problem. We have already mentioned above such conditions as psychopathy, hysteria and homosexuality. Sometimes though these can be at the root of the lack of due discretion as a ground for nullity, but by the same token they can also (though not necessarily) be at the root of a person's inability to assume the obligations of marriage. Below will be found two cases which will illustrate the conditions of psychopathy and hysteria as forming the basis for the person's inability to assume the obligations of marriage.

However it will also be quite clear that the evidence which is collected concerning these states must, where possible, show the character and personality prior to the marriage; and then detail the precise behavioural pattern after the marriage. Moreover the statements of the petitioner must be clearly supported and corroborated by such evidence. But if and when it is and the condition is seen to be serious, then it may be possible for the judges to conclude that the person was unable to assume the obligations of marriage.

*Case of nullity on the grounds of the inability to assume the obligations of marriage (psychopathy)*

Angela met Rowland at the 21st birthday party of her sister. At this time she was twenty-three and Rowland twenty-four. He was tall, handsome, very charming, though inclined to be a little distant at times. The couple saw each other a few times a week for a period of a year. He appeared to be kind and attentive, and very polite to her parents. He seemed to have plenty of money, though he was always reticent about where he worked and what he did; but Angela concluded that he had something to do with selling cars. The courtship progressed and they became engaged. Only two events caused any disturbance during this time. One was after the couple had selected an engagement ring, and Rowland had collected it from the jewellers; he had left the car parked in the street, and on returning he said he had found the car had been broken into and the ring stolen. In any event they were able to claim on their insurance for the price of the ring. The other event was when Rowland had had several drinks at a party, and had become very aggressive and unpleasant to his own brother who had been larking about. The wedding went off well; but on the honeymoon Rowland discovered that he had left his wallet behind (with all their money). However Angela was able to pay the bills with her cheque book, which sums Rowland was to return to her when they got home. On the honeymoon Rowland did not seem to be very gentle at intercourse, but Angela put this down to his (and her) inexperience. On returning home, the couple set about painting and decorating their newly acquired flat; and it was at this time that Angela discovered that Rowland had left his job. He said it was because he wanted to look for something with more of a future as well as more money. Whilst he was looking for a suitable job, Angela was working and supporting them both. Rowland did not seem to be in any great hurry to find a job, though she put this down to the fact that he was anxious to find the right one. She suggested to him that perhaps for the time being he might take any job that would bring in some money, and meanwhile look for the right job, answering advertisements. Rowland did not think this was the right approach at all; but then discovered what he thought would be the ideal work—collaborating with a man who was writing a film script. He therefore began working at home, but also asked Angela to lend him £250 to put into the venture as his share of the capital. She felt that to eat into their savings this way would be unwise, and gently refused. At this stage he became violent; and indeed on every subsequent occasion when he could not get his own way he resorted to violence.

He also started staying out at night, and then for periods of several days at a stretch; and he accounted for his absences by telling Angela that he was working with his partner on selecting shooting locations for the forthcoming film. Knowing nothing of the film business she believed him to start with; but then his general attitude towards her, his violence, his lack of earning anything at all (and yet apparently being able to find money for drinking and eating meals away from home)—all this began to make her doubt him. Occasions of violence were followed by episodes of deep remorse, with assurances that he would do better in the future. However the situation at home was becoming desperate; and then Angela became pregnant. This seemed to anger Rowland even more, and his violence towards her, even in that condition, increased. She threatened to leave him, and there was a further scene with tears in which he protested that he could not live without her. He even threatened suicide if she left him. Finally the time came when she would have to leave work, and there was still no sign of him improving, so she did indeed leave him and returned to her parents. He took to haunting the parents' home, threatening alternately violence to his wife and her parents or suicide. Eventually the police

had to be called to restrain him. Subsequently, Angela divorced
Rowland (alleging cruelty and unreasonable behaviour) and then
petitioned for a decree of nullity, alleging Rowland's inability to
assume the obligations of marriage. The story she told was
corroborated to the hilt and the grounds were proved, and a decree
was issued.

*Case of nullity on the grounds of the inability to assume the obligations
of marriage (hysteria)*

Charles met Daphne at a New Year's eve Ball. The couple began
to go out together; and Charles was deeply attracted towards the
girl. She was very beautiful, dressed extremely well, in the fashion,
but she was not unknown to 'dress to attract' wearing fairly low cut
dresses, and very short mini-skirts. She was the life and soul of the
party, and invariably had a circle of male admirers in attendance on
such occasions. She was a forthright girl and spoke her mind.
All this appeared to Charles to be very captivating. His sister who
met Daphne took an instant dislike to her, but could not tell her
brother why. In some ways Daphne appeared to be somewhat flirty
and coquettish, and appeared to be quite ready to have intercourse
before the marriage. An engagement took place, and there were a
few rows between the couple (on one occasion Daphne threw the
ring back at Charles over some tiny incident of no importance
whatsoever). After the marriage, the couple went on their
honeymoon but from the very start she did not appear to be keen on
the intimacies of married life; and indeed after two occasions
of intercourse on the honeymoon, it became infrequent:
Charles also noticed that Daphne appeared to be very jealous
of him from the start; he did not give her cause for this, but she
would act in a jealous and suspicious fashion when he so much as
gave the time of day to a member of the opposite sex in their hotel.
When they returned home to their newly acquired flat Charles was
pleased to see that Daphne immediately took up with one of their
neighbours, and was very close to her. However he was very
surprised when he returned home one day to hear Daphne referring
to her close friend and neighbour in bitter and spiteful terms. It
emerged that the two women had had a small disagreement about
the shopping; and from that moment onwards Daphne cut the
neighbour and refused to speak to her. At the same time Charles'
wife took up with another neighbour and was extremely close to
her; but their friendship soon ended. The situation with the
neighbours was now very embarrassing; since if Charles was
observed by Daphne to bid good morning to either of them she
refused to speak to him for several days. Eventually Charles had to

think of moving their flat to escape the embarrassment. In other ways Daphne acted strangely as well; she appeared to suffer from very frequent aches and pains; and specially a painful neck. Doctors were consulted and no help could be given; until finally one consultant suggested seeing a neurologist or a psychiatrist because he doubted that there was anything physically wrong with Daphne. This infuriated her, and she refused to see the consultant again, even darkly hinting at some impropriety that he had committed when she last saw him. Apart from all this, the relationship between the married couple was impossible. In a sunny mood, Daphne could change in a flash; and Charles never knew when he returned home in the evening how he would find her. When they did have rows, Daphne raised her voice to such a pitch that her husband feared she might become hysterical. Finally he discovered that she was having a relationship with an Insurance Agent who collected at the door. This was the last straw for Charles and he took advice from his doctor, a psychiatrist and a priest; and all told him that he would never be able to live with Daphne, and to leave her before his own health (which had become precarious) broke down completely. Subsequently a divorce was granted to Daphne; and Charles petitioned for a decree of nullity on the grounds of Daphne's inability to assume the obligations of marriage. Evidence showed that she was childish, immature, spoiled; and that she suffered from a serious hysterical personality disorder. In the light of the evidence, and that this was a condition from which she suffered from before the marriage, the grounds were found to be proved; and a decree of nullity granted.

We have now concluded our very brief treatment of those grounds for nullity which demand a formal process, and which relate in some way to the consent to be given by both parties to the union or to their ability to evaluate or assume the obligations of marriage. In the next chapter we will deal with the diriment impediments which are set out in the *Code of Canon Law* and briefly indicate where the grounds of nullity exist. Certain of these marriage impediments require a merely administrative process to show their existence, and therefore the nullity of marriage. Others require a formal process. After dealing with impediments, we will then go on to explain the two ways in which a nullity case is dealt with: the formal nullity trial, and the informal administrative process.

## Chapter 5

## THE GROUNDS FOR NULLITY – DIRIMENT IMPEDIMENTS

Most people have a vague idea of what an impediment is—for example, they appreciate that a man cannot marry his sister. Although in everyday terms such a union would be ruled out by the fact that sexual intercourse between a brother and sister is incest, the technical expression for the embargo on such a union is a *diriment impediment*—in this case, of consanguinity. An impediment is some fact or situation which prohibits two persons from marrying. Some of these impediments *merely* prohibit a couple from marrying, although if they did marry (e.g. two Catholics in the Church before a priest and two witnesses), the union would probably be valid, though it would be gravely unlawful. There are other impediments which not only prohibit certain couples from marrying, but also mean that any union which does take place in spite of the impediment would be null and void.

There are a number of diriment impediments (i.e. ones which make a marriage null and void). Some of these are regarded as having their origin in the Divine Law; others are regarded as originating from ecclesiastical law. It should be recalled at this point that since the Church has been founded by Christ as the means of grace for all mankind, and as the means through which the grace of the Sacraments is conferred, the Church has also been made competent by Christ to establish certain rules and regulations relating to the reception and conferring of the Sacraments. Marriage is a sacrament, and therefore it is subject to the rules established by the Church. Sometimes these impediments of ecclesiastical law have their basis in Divine Law, which the Church has then somewhat extended for good reasons. Others have their origin wholly and entirely in ecclesiastical law, for reasons of fitness or suitability, or perhaps sometimes for the good of the members of the Church.

The purpose of this chapter may puzzle the reader since it will be thought that if two Catholics marry in the Church, they must be free of impediments or they would not have been allowed to marry in the first place. To a large extent this is true. In these days, before a marriage can take place in the Catholic Church, there is what is called the *pre-nuptial enquiry* form to be completed by each party, and this form is designed to find out whether any impediments exist. Where an impediment comes to light, provided it is of a kind which can be dispensed, and which is in fact dispensed, then the marriage can validly and lawfully take place in the Church. But there are some impediments which are less obvious than others, and there may be a chance that such an impediment is not noticed or disclosed at the time of the pre-marriage investigation. When such a situation does occur, there are two possible courses open. If the impediment is one which can be dispensed, the couple have the option of seeking the dispensation and then of renewing their consent (before a priest and two witnesses—as in the case of a normal marriage), or they may separate. But if the impediment is one which cannot be dispensed, then the couple would not have the alternative of renewing their consent and remaining together.

The word dispensation means the relaxation of the law in a particular case by which permission is granted by the proper authority, and which thereby allows the valid celebration of marriage. But of course, there are certain impediments from which no dispensation can be granted. For example, the impediment of the particular degree of consanguinity which prevents a man marrying his sister cannot be dispensed. The reason for this has already been mentioned. There are certain impediments of the *Divine Law* which cannot be dispensed by any earthly authority. Only impediments of ecclesiastical law can be dispensed if the reasons brought forward are good enough.

Where the matter of diriment impediments is also relevant is that some of these impediments are regarded as applying to non-Catholics. Consequently, if two non-Catholics marry but there exists some impediment which invalidates their union, then this union could be declared null and void, provided that proof was brought forward by one of the parties. Thus, certain impediments can affect both Catholics and non-Catholics. What this means to our present study is that it may be possible to show that an undispensed diriment impediment existed, thus invalidating a marriage. If this impediment can be established according to the requirements of the law, then such a union could be declared null and void. There are two sorts of nullity process, both of which will be dealt with fully in the following chapters. One process, called the *formal nullity process*, is the kind used for cases in which it is alleged that there was some defect of consent. This process is also used for establishing the existence of impediments which may take some considerable degree of proof. The other kind of process—the *informal or administrative process*—is used in the case of other impediments whose existence can be established solely from documents. We will deal with all the impediments together. In the first group we will concentrate on those which may require the formal process; in the second group we will mention those which may be dealt with by means of the informal or administrative procedure.

## I DIRIMENT IMPEDIMENTS WHICH MAY REQUIRE PROOF BY FORMAL NULLITY PROCESS

AGE

The current law of the Church stipulates that a valid marriage cannot be contracted by a boy until he has passed his sixteenth birthday, and by a girl until she has passed her fourteenth birthday. This law hardly affects England and Wales where, by civil law, no marriage may take place before either party is sixteen, and even after this parental permission is required up to a certain age for a marriage to take place. In this respect, the practical rules for the marriage of Catholics are that the civil law must be observed.

However, outside England and Wales, different civil laws are in force. It is necessary, therefore, to appreciate that there are some places in which marriage can take place, even before the age of sixteen. But the canonical rule applies to all baptized people, hence if any marriage takes place in which one or both the parties are under age and baptized and no dispensation has been granted, it could be shown to be invalid.

This impediment of lack of age (or nonage) is one of ecclesiastical origin. This accounts for the fact that the bishop may dispense the lack of age up to one year. The natural law requires that the parties have sufficient knowledge and discretionary ability concerning the obligations of marriage, as well as the ability to assume them, in order to marry validly. Though the unbaptized are not bound by the laws of the Church, they are bound by the natural law. Therefore, although strictly speaking the impediment of nonage does not apply to the unbaptized, they are bound by the requirements of the natural law to marry validly. Although normally speaking the unbaptized would not be subject to a nullity procedure, were this to happen and the lack of age were to be alleged, then it would be necessary to show that the natural law requirements were not fulfilled (as mentioned above). The actual impediment of nonage could not be alleged. As it will be seen later, however, were a case involving an unbaptized person to be brought forward, it would more than likely be dealt with by means of a totally different procedure (i.e. the dissolution in favour of the faith).

ABDUCTION

This is not an impediment which has very much relevance today, though it has been known to occur in the past in Europe and the United States. From the accounts of Rotal trials, it seems that such cases occurred frequently in the opening years of the century. The law states that if a woman has been abducted by a man with a view to marriage, a diriment impediment exists invalidating such a marriage whilst the girl remains in the power of her abductor. Moreover, violent detention of a girl is regarded as equivalent to abduction.

Abduction is the violent removal of a woman from a safe place to a place which is not safe. It is necessary that the girl be removed by force or deceit. If she goes willingly, even though against the wishes of her parents or guardian, there would be no impediment. Thus, a couple who elope to Gretna Green would not find there is a diriment impediment which forbids (and invalidates their subsequent) marriage in a church, since it is assumed in an elopement that both parties go quite willingly.

This impediment is of ecclesiastical law, and therefore, following the normal rules, it only binds the baptized. The impediment ceases to exist when the girl is returned to a safe place, which is out of the power of her abductor. A subsequent marriage would be valid provided that the girl freely consents. This impediment is not generally dispensed because the bishop would always insist that the girl is returned to a safe place, and the impediment ceases once the girl has been set free from the power of the man who abducted her. Thus, there is no call for the dispensation to be granted. It will be appreciated that this is an impediment which is hardly likely to arise in this country.


CRIME

The name of this impediment is misleading. The term crime has a very specialised meaning in the present context. There are three forms or degrees of this impediment[1]. Firstly, there is the situation in which during a valid marriage of a couple, one of the spouses commits adultery, and with this third person exchanges a promise to attempt marriage, even only a civil marriage. The impediment prevents the spouse of the marriage and the third party from marrying even after the death of the other spouse of the valid marriage.

---

[1]    Though it is proposed in the new Code to reduce these three degrees to one only, namely the last of those mentioned here.

To explain this, an example will be helpful. Anne and Peter are validly married, but the marriage seems to be falling apart. Peter begins to go out with Sonia, with whom he commits adultery. They agree to marry after Anne (suffering from cancer) has died. Not long afterwards Anne does die. However, there exists an impediment (of crime) which prevents Peter and Sonia marrying validly. If they do attempt to marry, their union would be invalid in the eyes of the Church, unless the impediment of crime is dispensed.

Essential points concerning this impediment are these. There must be true intercourse between Peter and Sonia. If Sonia does not realise that Peter is married at the time, then the impediment does not arise—that is, the third party must be *aware* that he or she is involved in an act of *adultery*. The impediment also arises if, after the adultery (even without a promise of marriage), a divorce is obtained and Peter 'marries' Sonia during the lifetime of Anne. The impediment would prevent the valid marriage of Peter and Sonia, even after the death of Anne. However, for this form of the impediment, the local bishop has the power to dispense.

The second form or degree of the impediment of crime arises when, during the lifetime of the existing spouse, the other spouse commits adultery, and one of them (the other spouse or the third party) kills the remaining spouse. To illustrate this with our example: Peter is married to Anne. During the marriage Peter and Sonia commit adultery. Thereafter, because they wish to marry each other, they plan to, and do, kill Anne. The dispensation from this second form of the impediment of crime is much more difficult to obtain.

The third form of this impediment arises when even though there has been no adultery, one of the spouses and a third party mutually co-operate in the killing of the other spouse. To illustrate this, Peter, being validly married to Anne, co-operates physically or morally with Sonia in the murder of Anne. The impediment arises so that if Peter and Sonia try to marry after Anne's death, their marriage would be invalid. If the murder (and the identity of the culprits) is public knowledge, the Church does not dispense the impediment. Where the facts are entirely secret and there is no likelihood of the truth becoming known generally, then the Church might in certain very grave circumstances, dispense the impediment.

It will be seen why this impediment, of ecclesiastical origin, was introduced into the law by the Church. Adultery with a promise of marriage, adultery with a civil marriage, coniugicide with or without adultery—these are acts which attack the very foundation of married life. It is entirely proper that such conduct should be condemned by the Church, and the means she uses here is the establishment of the impediment of crime. It should be noted, however, that this impediment, because it is one of the ecclesiastical law only, affects only the baptized, and not two unbaptized persons.

PUBLIC PROPRIETY

This is an impediment which originates in ecclesiastical law. It arises from an invalid marriage (whether consummated or not), and it also can arise from 'public or notorious concubinage'. This is an impediment which is very like that of affinity (with which we will deal shortly). The impediment invalidates a marriage between a man and the grandmother, mother, daughter or granddaughter of the woman with whom he is 'living'. An example will illustrate the impediment.

David is living with (or married invalidly by reason of some impediment, to) Helen. There is an impediment to marriage if David tries to contract a union with Helen's mother or grand-mother, or with Helen's daughter or granddaughter. In technical terms, marriage is prohibited and invalidated between David and the blood relations of Helen (with whom he is living) in the direct line in the first and second degree. We will see how the relationship between two people is calculated in the direct and collateral line when we deal with consanguinity and affinity.

The impediment will arise between two people who are bound to the form of marriage (e.g. two Catholics) who marry invalidly and live together. But for the impediment to exist, it is necessary for there to be some semblance of a marriage, one which is, however, invalid by reason of some impediment, or defective consent. The impediment is of ecclesiastical law only, and therefore does not bind the unbaptized when they marry amongst themselves. It is sometimes possible, for serious and grave reasons, to obtain a dispensation from this impediment.

LEGAL RELATIONSHIP

This impediment is a good example of Church law following the civil law in certain matters. Those who are disqualified from marrying by civil law as a result of some legal relationship arising from adoption, are also prohibited by ecclesiastical law from marrying, and any such attempted union would be invalid. In Britain, there is a legal prohibition against an adoptive parent marrying the adopted child. Although, technically, the Church has the power to dispense this impediment, it would not do so in places where the civil law forbade such marriages.

IMPOTENCE

This is an impediment of the natural law. Church law states the impediment thus: Antecedent and perpetual impotence, whether on the part of the man or the woman, whether known or unknown, whether absolute or relative, invalidates the marriage by the law of nature itself. Sterility, however, does not invalidate a marriage. In simple terms, impotence can be described as the inability to perform the marital act, whereas sterility would be described as the incapacity for generation. Thus, if a couple are able to have normal intercourse, but because of some condition in either or both of them they cannot have children, this is the condition canonically termed *sterility*. But if the couple are unable to have normal intercourse, this is termed *impotence*. Unfortunately, having made this comparatively simple distinction, it is extremely difficult, in fact, to distinguish between the two in many concrete cases.

There are, therefore, a series of terms to be explained as they are understood in Canon Law. Intercourse is defined as the penetration of the vagina by the male organ, with the ejaculation of male seed in the vagina. Where this is not possible, then there exists the condition of impotence. For this reason, if it is not possible for the male to penetrate the vagina, or if the male is not capable of sustaining an erection, or if he is not able to ejaculate semen within the vagina, he is regarded as impotent. If the female does not have a vagina at all, or if it is too small, so as to prevent penetration, she is regarded as impotent. The jurisprudence of the Sacred Roman Rota on this important matter is the basic guide for all local tribunals in endeavouring to assess whether one of the parties in a particular case is impotent.

The impediment of impotence exists if it is a condition antecedent to the marriage, and perpetual. Antecedent impotence involves the condition existing at the time of the marriage and beforehand. Perpetual impotence implies a condition which cannot be cured by means which are licit and not dangerous to life. For example, if a man's impotent condition could be cured, but by means of an operation which would place the man in serious danger, his condition would be regarded, canonically, as beyond the ordinary means of remedy, and hence the condition would be described as permanent.

Absolute impotence refers to that condition which exists regardless of the partner involved—that is, the person would be impotent regardless of his partner. Relative impotence exists where a person is impotent with one person, but would not necessarily be so with another. This type of condition—relative impotence— exists particularly where say, the wife from the very day of the marriage has a horror of her husband, and becomes tense or completely frigid if he attempts to touch her. Relative impotence is most frequently present when there are psychological troubles affecting one or both partners.

Impotence is an impediment of the natural law. That is to say, it affects both the baptized and the unbaptized. The reason for this wide extension of the impediment is that, since the transference of the rights to procreation of children should be exchanged by the partners with each other, if one of the partners cannot have intercourse, he is not conferring upon his wife the rights to conjugal acts[1]. Naturally this is not his own fault, but since he does not have the ability to transfer these rights to his partner, he is unable to marry. That is, speaking in terms of contractual law, the person lacks the necessary 'consideration' which is vital for a contract to be made. On the other hand, sterility does not invalidate a marriage. A person who is sterile, a woman who has passed through the change of life, or a woman who has had her ovaries removed, or a man who does not have an adequate sperm-count—all of these can marry, since their condition of sterility is not the same as the inability to have intercourse.

The proof of this impediment can be a problem principally because it is often very difficult to establish that the condition existed at the time of marriage. The reason is that, normally, if a person knew about the condition, it is unlikely that he would have married, or that his wife would have accepted him in marriage. On the other hand, if he did not know about the condition, for this very reason there would be no expert or medical witnesses to the condition. It is for this reason, too, that there are special provisions made in Canon Law for a case such as this to be changed into a petition for the dispensation of a non-consummated marriage.

One further point is important. The civil law on this matter is rather different from Canon Law, and for this reason the situation can become confused. In civil law, there are grounds for annulment if a partner to the union was unable or unwilling to consummate. There is no ground for nullity of *impotence,* so-called. In Canon Law impotence *is* a ground for nullity. However, where a marriage is alleged to be unconsummated, and a plea is made to the Holy Father on this count, the petition is for a *dispensation* of the marriage (not a declaration of nullity) on the grounds of non-consummation. It will be seen, therefore, that there are considerable differences on this point between the two forms of law.

---

[1]    Impotence can of course affect either of the partners.

## II  THOSE DIRIMENT IMPEDIMENTS WHICH MAY BE DEALT WITH BY MEANS OF AN ADMINISTRATIVE PROCESS

Before dealing with the second group of impediments, we must mention again the reason for making the distinction between these two groups. Basically, the reason is that this second group can be dealt with (to establish their existence and thereby show a marriage to be invalid) very much more easily, as will be seen in the next chapter. The procedure merely demands that the impediment is shown to exist by means of certain and authentic documents according to the special norms of the law. Bearing this point in mind, it will be seen that the following impediments are all capable of being demonstrated through written documents rather than by formal verbal evidence.

THE IMPEDIMENT OF PRIOR MARRIAGE OR 'LIGAMEN'

A person who is bound by the bond of a valid marriage may not contract a further marriage. If he does attempt a second union, it would be invalid. On the other hand, it may be possible to declare the first union to be invalid for some reason, in which case it will be possible for the person concerned to marry, provided that the nullity (or dispensation from an unconsummated union or dissolution of a non-sacramental union) has been properly established according to the laws of the Church.

This impediment is usually most complicated when first examined, but with appropriate documents its existence can be declared fairly speedily. An example will illustrate the impediment. Henry marries Rachel. Both are baptized non-Catholics and they marry in their local Anglican parish church. The marriage is not happy and Rachel leaves Henry, divorces him, and then marries— this time in the register office—Raymond, also a baptized non-Catholic. This marriage likewise disintegrates, and Raymond falls in love with Susan, a Roman Catholic. Provided it can be shown that Henry validly married Rachel, it follows that there is the impediment of a prior marriage or *ligamen* which invalidates the marriage of Rachel and Raymond. Hence, Raymond is free to marry Susan.

This impediment is one of the Divine Law, and therefore it binds even the unbaptized. In the above example, the impediment ceases to exist between Rachel and Raymond when Henry dies. Thus if Rachel and Raymond marry after Henry's death, their union would be regarded as valid. Raymond would not then be free to marry Susan. More attention will be given to this matter in the next chapter, when dealing with the actual process for the establishment of the impediment.

THE IMPEDIMENT OF DISPARITY OF CULT

This impediment is of ecclesiastical law, and binds only Roman Catholics. By this impediment, a marriage which takes place between a person bound to the form of Catholic marriage and a person who has not been baptized, without the necessary dispensation, is invalid. This means that a person who has been baptized in, or at least receive into, the Catholic Church (whether as an infant or as a convert) cannot validly marry an unbaptized person unless the necessary dispensation has been granted.

As mentioned above, the impediment binds only Catholics marrying unbaptized persons. It does not affect the status of the marriage of a baptized non-Catholic who marries an unbaptized person. This is an impediment which does not figure largely in the work of marriage tribunals. Indeed, at present it is almost impossible for a marriage to take place without the dispensation unless the priest concerned forgets to apply for it, or unless the priest illegally celebrates the marriage without the dispensation. The normal way in which the invalidating effects of this impediment are averted is this. Whenever a Catholic wishes to marry a non-Catholic, the latter is asked to obtain a copy of his baptismal certificate. If this cannot be found, then more enquiries are made to discover whether perhaps the person was never baptized. Even when the non-Catholic does produce a baptismal certificate, in some dioceses in the present day the Vicar General grants a dispensation from mixed religion (the non-invalidating impedi- existing when a Catholic and a baptized non-Catholic wish to marry), but at the same time there is also issued, as a precaution (in case the baptism never took place, or in case it was not valid), a dispensation from the impediment of disparity of cult.


THE IMPEDIMENT OF HOLY ORDERS

The basis of this impediment is that a cleric who is in major Orders—Priesthood or Diaconate—cannot validly marry unless the impediment has been dispensed by the appropriate authority. The Church does dispense the impediment in the case of deacons, without too much difficulty. But though she also dispenses the impediment of the priesthood, this dispensation is not granted easily or readily, and it is only given after most careful examination of the case. Even so, when the Holy See has dispensed the impediment of the priesthood and thereby enables an ex-priest to marry, this union, although a sacrament, and taking place with the blessing of the Church, must be celebrated very quietly, and without fuss and public show. The reasons are obvious.

THE IMPEDIMENT OF SOLEMN VOWS

The impediment of solemn vows is much the same as that of Holy Orders. What is forbidden is for a person to marry who has taken solemn vows. Such vows are those which are taken by religious like Benedictines, Franciscans, Passionists and certain orders of nuns. There is a slight exception to this rule however. One religious order, the Society of Jesus, normally only has simple vows, which are taken by Jesuits after their lengthy novitiate. These also preclude the person concerned from marrying. The impediment invalidating marriage ceases to exist when the person concerned has been dispensed by the Holy See. Again, this is something that is not done lightly, for obvious reasons.

THE IMPEDIMENT OF CONSANGUINITY

Consanguinity is the impediment which exists between blood relations. The impediment can exist in what is called the *collateral line*, which is the relationship between brothers and sisters, between cousins, between uncle and niece, etc. The relationship can also exist in the *direct line*, which is the connection between a mother and son, or grandmother and grandson, and the like. The best method of establishing the relationship that exists between two persons is to plot some kind of genealogical tree. The lines running up and down are in the direct line; those running off as branches are in the collateral line. But to complicate the matter, there are also degrees of relationship. For example, there is a closer relationship between brother and sister, than there is between two cousins. To be able to plot the degree of relationship it is necessary to establish the common ancestor which exists in a particular case. For example, Henry is the father of Peter and Paul. Henry is the common ancestor. The degree of relationship existing between the two brothers is decided by counting the number of generations back to, but not counting, the common ancestor. Thus in the case of Peter and Paul, there is one generation back to Henry, their father. Hence, Peter and Paul are connected in the *first degree,* and since this relationship is one concerning the branches stemming from the common ancestor, their relationship is in the *collateral line.* Then Peter and Paul have children. Peter is the father of Mary, and Paul is the father of Robert. The relationship between Robert and Mary is decided by counting the generations back to Henry, the common ancestor. There are two such generations, not counting Henry. Hence, the relationship is described as being in the *second degree* of the collateral line.

There is an added complication where the generations back to the common ancestor are not equal. For instance the relationship between Paul and Mary is that of uncle to niece. The way this is described in Canon Law is to mention the number of generations on the longer line first, and relating this to the number of generations on the shorter line. Thus the relationship between Paul and Mary is that of the *second degree* (on Mary's side) *touching the first* (on Paul's side), in the collateral line. In the *direct* line, the relationship between Henry and Mary is that of the *second degree* in the *direct* line, since there are two generations from Mary to Henry, not counting Henry.

This is a complicated impediment, but it can easily be resolved by drawing a genealogical tree, and this will also show where there are more complex relationships: for example, where two cousins are related not only on their father's side, but also on their mother's side. The law of the Church on the matter is that consanguinity existing in the *direct line* (either ascending or descending) constitutes a diriment impediment. In the *collateral line,* marriage is invalid by reason of the impediment of consanguinity up to the third degree. Therefore, marriage between any relatives in the direct line (mother and son, grandmother and grandson, etc) is invalid. In the collateral line, a marriage between brother and sister, first and second cousins is invalid. However, the relationship between third cousins is not a *diriment* impediment[1].

The origin of the impediment of consanguinity depends on the nature of the relationship. It is considered that consanguinity in the *direct line* is an impediment of the Divine Law, in the first degree, and some authors regard other degrees also as of the Divine Law though this is not so certain. If it is not an impediment of the Divine Law for these other degrees, it is most certainly an impediment of the ecclesiastical law, and for these direct line relationships the Church does not generally grant dispensations.

In the collateral line, most authors regard the relationship between brother and sister as an impediment of the Divine Law; in all other degrees of the collateral line (i.e. between first cousins and less), it is an impediment of ecclesiastical law. The unbaptized are not bound by the impediments which are *certainly* considered to be merely of the ecclesiastical law. Where there exists an impediment which is not certainly of the Divine Law between two non-baptized persons, the marriage would, normally, be regarded as valid. However, since the unbaptized are bound not by ecclesiastical law, but by the civil laws of the place where they live, the point hardly

---

[1]    In the proposed new Code, the method of computing relationships in the collateral line has been altered. However the only practical difference which may be made by the promulgation of the new Code (here) will be that no longer is there a diriment impediment concerning second cousins.

need concern us here. The Church does not dispense from the impediment in the first degree of the collateral line, but she will dispense for urgent and serious reasons lesser degrees of relationship. Nonetheless, since serious effects can sometimes ensue from intermarriage, such dispensations are not easily given.

### THE IMPEDIMENT OF AFFINITY

This is the impediment that arises between one party of a marriage and the blood relations of the other. Thus, for example, there is a relationship of affinity between a man and the sisters of his wife. This impediment only arises from a valid marriage. The degrees of relationship can be shown by means of an example. Rupert and Sarah marry. Rupert is related by affinity to the sisters of Sarah. Since Sarah and her sisters are related in the first degree of the collateral line of consanguinity, there is also the relationship of the first degree of the collateral line of affinity between Rupert and Sarah's sisters. Similarly, Rupert is related to his first cousin Michael by the second degree of the collateral line of consanguinity. Therefore, Sarah is related to Michael in the second degree of the collateral line of affinity. The rule is that the same degree of *affinity* exists between Rupert and the blood relations of Sarah as there exists in a relationship of consanguinity between Sarah and her blood relations.

This impediment is one of ecclesiastical law, and therefore affects only the baptized. However, when an unbaptized person wishes to marry a baptized person, he becomes subject to the impediment if it exists. The Church hardly ever dispenses from affinity in the direct line when the marriage of the two spouses has been consummated. If the marriage has not been consummated, the dispensation is less difficult to obtain. For affinity in the collateral line, the impediment is fairly easily obtained for a good reason. The law of the Church states that there is a diriment impediment where affinity exists in the direct line in all degrees. The impediment is diriment in the collateral line up to the second degree—for example, between a man and the first cousin of his wife[1]. This is also a complicated impediment to determine, and some skill is required to work it out accurately.

### THE IMPEDIMENT OF SPIRITUAL RELATIONSHIP

When a person is baptized, there arises a *spiritual relationship* between this person and the one who baptizes him, and also between the baptized person and his godparents. Thus there arises

---

[1] The new Code proposes to restrict the impediment of affinity in the collateral line to the relationship between a man and his deceased wife's sister.

a spiritual relationship between the priest and the baby whom he baptizes, and also between the godparents and the baby. This impediment rarely creates any problems with regard to marriage, since there will probably be some twenty or so years between the baby and his spiritual relations. However, the situation can become more relevant when it involves the marriage of an adult received into the Church with absolute baptism.

For this impediment of spiritual relationship to arise, it is necessary for the godparents and the one baptizing also to be baptized, and it is necessary that the baptism is absolute and not merely conditional. When a proxy stands in for the real godparent, the relationship arises not between the baptized person and the proxy, but with the proper godparent. An example of when this impediment arises can be given. A young man has been led to the faith by the good example of his girl friend, and as a result he takes instruction. He is ready to be received, and since he has never been baptized before he is baptized absolutely. If the girl friend stands as sponsor for the young man at his baptism, the diriment impediment of spiritual relationship arises between them, and this prevents them from marrying unless the impediment is dispensed. Happily the impediment is quite easily dispensed if there are good enough reasons. The impediment does not arise between the godparents and the one baptized in non-Catholic churches[1].

We have now concluded our examination of the impediments which invalidate marriage. The point of mentioning them here is that if a diriment impediment does exist, it may be possible to show that the marriage under examination is null and void. We will now move on to examine the two types of nullity procedure that exist in the Church: the formal and the administrative types. All those grounds of nullity examined in the earlier chapters together with the first group of impediments dealt with here are considered under the formal procedure, whilst the impediments mentioned in the second group above are dealt with by the administrative procedure.

---

[1]    The proposed new Code has eliminated the impediment of spiritual relationship from the law; moreover there is a fairly strong canonical view that with the introduction of the new rite of Baptism, the impediment has already been removed.

# Chapter 6

# PROCEDURE IN A NULLITY CASE—
# THE TRIBUNAL AND ITS OFFICIALS

Every nullity case involves two distinct elements: one is the evaluation and assessment of the evidence—the presumptions that may be drawn from certain facts, and the type of proof that is required. This element falls under the heading of jurisprudence. The guide lines here in any nullity case are taken principally from the Rotal Jurisprudence. This is a series of decisions of the Sacred Roman Rota which are published in shortened form some ten years after the actual decision itself was given. We will discuss the Rota later in this chapter. The other element that is involved in every nullity case is the procedure. The rules of procedure for each case are contained in outline in the *Code of Canon Law,* but there are fuller and much more specific rules given in an Instruction of the Sacred Congregation for the Discipline of the Sacraments. The Instruction is known by its first three words, *Provida Mater Ecclesia,* and it was issued on 15 August 1936.

Added to this there is a further group of regulations, some of them taking the place of the directions of *Provida Mater.* These additional regulations are contained in the *motu proprio* of Pope Paul VI called *Causas Matrimoniales* issued on 28 March 1971. The principal aim of this document was to speed up the processing of nullity cases, and specially of the treatment of appeals, which will be dealt with shortly. When the new *Code of Canon Law* is promulgated, this will incorporate most of the changes that have been made in the procedural law since the time of the progonal *Code of Canon Law* in 1918.

For centuries now, each diocese has had its own marriage tribunal, and in most areas these diocesan tribunals still exist. Where they do not, it is because a rather better system of regional tribunals has been introduced. It seems that the regional type of tribunal will certainly be more usual in the future. We will go into more detail about these shortly. However, what we now say relates equally to regional tribunals (with some few modifications) and to diocesan tribunals. The term tribunal has two senses. In the first sense, it is a department of the Diocesan *Curia* which looks after the day-to-day administration of marriage cases (not merely nullity cases, but also cases dealing with non-baptism and non-consummation).

The business of the tribunal is presided over by an experienced canon lawyer called the *officialis*. He makes the arrangements for prospective clients to be interviewed; for applications to be dealt with in the office; for evidence to be taken; for the personnel to be assigned to each case. He may well be assisted by a number of other priests and laity concerned with the administration of the cases; and he may also be helped by one of these other priests being constituted a *vice-officialis*. The *officialis* or 'president of the tribunal' has the same (ordinary) power in judicial matters as the Vicar General has in other matters.

There is the other, less proper, sense of the word tribunal. This sense covers the actual panel of priests, with their differing functions, who are actually concerned in dealing with one specific marriage case. In this sense, the tribunal is also called a court. Since, of course, there will be more than one nullity case being dealt with at any one time in the tribunal, there will also be a series of these courts in operation. Thus, it also follows that some of the priests involved in one court will also belong to other such courts. One priest can have any number of cases with which he is concerned, and hence he will be involved in as many courts as he has cases with which he is dealing. For each formal nullity case there will be a court of six persons as a minimum.

In each court there are three judges. These will be priests who are experienced in Canon Law, and some considerable experience in nullity work. One of these judges will be the 'president of the court', and he will generally be the person who manages the daily correspondence and detail connected with the case. Sometimes the president of the court will also be the *ponens*, the name given to the person who leads the discussion of the case at the decision hearing, and who eventually produces the lengthy *sentence* which presents the reasons in law and fact for the decision.

The court will also have a *defender of the bond of marriage*. He is a priest skilled in Canon Law, whose role it is to look after the interests of the bond of marriage. It will be appreciated that when someone petitions to have his marriage declared null and void, this person is impugning the validity of the marriage—that is, he is alleging that there is no marriage at all. The 'defender of the bond' represents the bond of marriage and brings forward arguments showing why the marriage should be regarded as valid. On the other side, each petitioner will be represented by an *advocate* who assists the petitioner to prepare his case. Towards the end of the proceedings, the advocate produces arguments showing why the marriage should be declared null and void. Hence, he and the 'defender of the bond' are on opposing sides. Both the 'defender of the bond' and the advocate will usually be priests, although there are some places (for example at the Sacred Roman Rota, and in at least one diocese in the United States) where the advocate is a layman. The advocate, if he is so appointed by the petitioner, can also act as the latter's proxy, so that certain documents can be signed, and some appearances can be made on behalf of the petitioner by the proxy. Finally, each court has a *notary,* also usually a priest who takes down the testimony at formal evidence sessions, and whose signature on the documents shows that the documents and other papers in the case are authentic. Sometimes, it may be necessary for another official called the *promotor of justice* to have some part in the proceedings. We will examine the function of this official in connection with our explanation of the court's proceedings later.

It is obvious that where a tribunal has a large volume of business, it will also be neccessary to have a considerable organization backing the officials. Today most large tribunals are backed by a staff of lay persons; as well as by all the necessary business mechanics and paraphernalia.

It is proposed to examine what happens in such a case from the time the very first inquiry is made until a declaration of nullity (or final rejection) is issued. A nullity case can originate in one of several ways. A case can begin with the person concerned consulting his parish priest. The priest would wisely refer the person directly to the tribunal for an expert opinion. Sometimes the first approach is made as a result of a visit to the Catholic Marriage Advisory Council. After some time spent examining the matter, it may be appreciated that nothing can be done to reconcile the partners to the broken marriage. Thereafter the person is referred to the appropriate tribunal. On other occasions, a person applies directly to a tribunal as a result of some advice from a friend, a solicitor, or maybe even a newspaper. However, when the first contact has been made, an appointment will be arranged and an interview will follow.

Different tribunals will have different methods of operation at this point. The interview with the prospective petitioner may be conducted by an advocate; or—in some places—it may be conducted by one of the number of judges who assist a tribunal. The purpose of having an interview with a judge rather than an advocate is based more on practicality than any matter of principle. It may be felt that a judge has more experience than the advocates; and would be able to spot the makings of a case quicker and get a case launched with less delay. In any event whoever the interview is with, it is the task of the president of the tribunal to ensure that a competent service of interviewing is available for prospective petitioners. When the interview has taken place, and there is a possibility of a case, as well as witnesses who may be able to give evidence about the grounds to be alleged, the interviewing priest would assist the client by drawing up a *libellus* or petition. The *libellus* signed by the petitioner—together with other supporting documents—is then presented formally to the tribunal (in the strict sense) for consideration.

When the tribunal receives the petition, the president, by virtue of certain powers that he enjoys, appoints a court composed of three judges, 'defender of the bond', advocate and notary. A decree appointing these persons is drawn up and signed by the president and authenticated by a notary. These are the officials of the court who will deal with this particular case throughout all its stages until the final decision as publication of the sentence.

The court, thus appointed, examines the petition to establish whether it can be accepted for trial. If it appears that the petition might have to be refused a trial or 'rejected', the three judges must discuss the case and the acceptance or rejection of the petition is agreed by majority vote. In either case, the petitioner is advised, and if the petition is rejected, the petitioner is also told the reasons.

The Canon Law on the matter of the rejection of petitions is quite clear. For the examination of the petition with a view to its acceptance or rejection, a number of points have to be considered. Firstly, the court's competence; secondly, whether the petitioner has the right to bring a case; thirdly, whether the case alleged has sufficient substance.

The ordinary competence[1] of any diocesan tribunal rests either upon the place where the marriage took place or the domicile of the respondent. Every court has to work upon certain laws of competence. For example, the English laws of competence for divorce courts are fairly strict. Similarly, the Church courts have to work according to fairly strict rules of competence.[2]

When the court has established that it is competent to try the case, it must next see whether the petitioner can be admitted to plead. The general rule is that any Catholic, provided that the rules of competence have been fulfilled, may plead a case as long as he is not a 'dishonourable petitioner'. This term refers to whether he was

[1]   Competence is the term given to the court's legal ability to accept and try the case, as opposed to the right of some other tribunal to do so.

[2]   Under the special rules of the document *Causas Matrimoniales,* it is possible for the tribunal in whose jurisdiction the bulk of the evidence will be collected to obtain competence from the place where the respondent lives.

the malicious cause of the nullity. If he was, then he is barred from pleading. For example, if the person before the marriage had deliberately prepared a series of documents showing that he did not intend to contract a permanent union, then he would certainly be regarded as the malicious cause of the alleged nullity. Generally, no petition could be accepted from him. This is a very proper provision, otherwise the very existence of ecclesiastical courts would tend to encourage people to contract impermanent unions. Sometimes, however, the bishop, having examined all the circumstances, may consider that though the petitioner was the deliberate cause of the alleged nullity, he is now so repentant of having thus acted that he may be allowed, as a special favour, to present a petition.

The third consideration is whether the petition submitted has sufficient substance. There are two, and only two, laws which govern this aspect of the acceptance of petitions. In fact the way the law is framed shows that the majority of cases should be admitted. The procedural rules are that the petition must be rejected: if the reasons alleged and other information submitted, even if proved and true, are not adequate to indicate that the marriage is null and void; or if, though the reasons alleged would be sufficient to show the marriage is null and void, the same reasons are nonetheless patently false or completely unprovable. An example of the former situation would be if the petitioner alleged nothing that could be construed as amounting to grounds for nullity. Such a petition would have to be rejected. An example of the second situation would be if the person alleged that his wife did not want children, but it was shown that the wife had already willingly had four children by him, and was hoping for a fifth. Again the petition would have to be rejected. Except for these two situations, the petition must be regarded as having some sort of substance, and it must be accepted for trial. Assuming that all these requirements have been satisfied, then a document is issued, indicating the acceptance.

One point that arises frequently is whether a non-Catholic can submit a petition to a marriage tribunal. As we have mentioned earlier, the Church is competent to deal with the examination of all marriages which are sacramental, and to pronounce on the validity of such union. Petitions from non-Catholics are not unusual, indeed frequent in cases where the non-Catholic wishes to re-marry a Catholic. The Church can, of course, deal with such cases just as easily as with cases presented by Catholics. The only slight difference is that, recognizing the fact that the petitioner is not a Catholic, it is necessary for the local bishop to give permission for the person concerned to plead before the tribunal. However, there is usually no difficulty about obtaining this permission.

The petition having been accepted for trial, the next requirement is that the other party—the respondent—should be informed of the ensuing proceedings. The technical term for this phase is the *citation*. Normally, this takes the form of a letter to the respondent advising him that his former partner has petitioned for the examination of the marriage and that the union has been alleged to be invalid on certain grounds. The respondent is also advised that there will be a meeting held in the near future at which the formal grounds for the alleged nullity will be agreed. He is asked to indicate whether he would like to intervene in the proceedings, and whether he would like to give evidence; or leave the whole matter to the court.

A reasonable length of time is allowed for the respondent to reply. Often the reply will be in the form of a document signed by the respondent indicating either that he wishes to be present at the first formal session of the court, or that he leaves the matter in the hands of the tribunal. If there is no reply after a reasonable length of time, another letter may be sent. If it is clear that the respondent has received the letters and has not replied, then the proceedings can commence, with a note entered into the documents of the case stating that the respondent has been cited, that so far as can be ascertained he has received the citation, but that he has not replied.

Assuming that the respondent has replied and has left the outcome of the case in the hands of the court, the court then meets for the first formal session at which the precise grounds of the alleged nullity are agreed. This is called the 'agreement of the point of issue', or in Latin, the *contestatio litis*. The agreement of the precise grounds upon which the nullity is sought is set down in a document which indicates the names of the members of the court. The petitioner is advised of all the persons involved, and is asked if he has any objection to them. The document also states the relevant details concerning the citation of the respondent, and the nature of his reply. Finally, the document sets down in a legal formula the actual grounds of the alleged nullity. The formula for a case in which the respondent has deliberately reserved to himself the right to obtain a divorce later in the marriage, would be more or less as follows: 'The point at issue was agreed by all present as: whether the marriage is null and void on the grounds of an intention *contra bonum sacramenti*'. This is the technical expression for an intention to exclude the permanence of marriage. This document is then signed by the judges, defender, proxy for the petitioner and notary.

Often, this meeting for the agreement of the point at issue is also chosen as the occasion when the evidence of the petitioner can be taken. Prior to the occasion when this testimony is obtained, the advocate has had the right to present a series of questions which he wishes to be asked of his client. These questions are handed to the 'defender of the bond' who has the responsibility for drawing up the questions in the case. The defender makes use of the questions already supplied by the advocate, and weaves them into his own questionnaire. At the evidence sessions, especially of the important witnesses such as the petitioner, respondent and others whose information might be critical to the whole case, there may be present at least one of the judges—usually the presiding judge—the 'defender of the bond' and the notary. By permission of the 'president of the court', the advocate may also be present.

It is important at this stage to emphasise that a canonical nullity process is a documentary one. Likewise, it is completely confidential. For this reason, there is no open court. There are no members of the public present, only those persons mentioned above together with the witness. Moreover, the method of taking evidence is not like that which is used in a civil court. There is no cross questioning, no oratory of advocates, no trying to discredit witnesses. 'Hearsay' is accepted into the evidence (though later on it is evaluated for what it is worth). The general pattern of an evidence session is one of much less formality than that which exists in civil courts. The interrogating judge first asks the preliminary questions, which deal with basic information such as names, address, profession, religion, status, and the like. The witness is asked to swear that he will will tell the truth, the whole truth, and nothing but the truth. Prior to this however, he is cautioned about the sacredness of an oath. Sometimes, there are occasions when a witness will not wish to take an oath on the Bible—he may only wish to 'affirm'. This is quite acceptable, though the point is noted for later evaluation.

The judge next puts the remaining and more special questions to the witness. Unlike the civil court, not every word that the witness says is taken down. More often than not, since the questions relate to extremely complicated issues such as people's intentions before marrying, some or even many years previously, the witness will be asked to *talk about* the matter for a little while, and then the judge will assist the witness to formulate an answer which contains the basic information sought by the court. It may be felt that this is not an ideal method of obtaining evidence. There can be the suspicion that because the judge assists the witness in formulating an answer it would not be the answer intended by the witness. However, as will be seen later on, the whole of the statement is read back to the witness at the end of the session, and on this occasion he has the opportunity of changing whatever he wishes in the testimony. In this way, at the end of the session, it is certain that what the deposition contains is precisely what the witness intended to say.

It is important to appreciate that the whole basis of a nullity case in an ecclesiastical court is different to that in the civil courts. In the latter type of process, the aim is to arrive at the truth through the clash of two opposites: of the plaintiff and of the defendant. Thus, in questioning witnesses in the civil courts, the lawyers put questions which they want precisely answered, in order that their case may be established. In cross-examination, certain of these answers are explained, or even explained away. On the other hand, the means of arriving at the truth in a church court is through searching investigation and enquiry. The inquiry is made by the judge in charge, not by those representing either side. Consequently, the judge is not so much interested in the 'yes' or 'no' type of answer to establish a 'case', but in *whatever* the witness says which will establish the truth.

When the judge is asking questions, he makes use of the material supplied by the 'defender of the bond'. But there are special rules which the defender must observe. For example, no question may be permitted which tends to trap the witness; no trick questions are allowed; and there may be no discrediting of witnesses. The judge has the responsibility of seeing that the questions remain within these confines. The judge is permitted to ask his own questions. He does this usually to elucidate a previous answer, or to cover some point that was not known about before the session began. Likewise, the 'defender of the bond' may wish to add further questions but he may do this only through the judge. He cannot ask the questions directly. In this way the cross-questioning of witnesses is avoided. The advocate, if he is present, may also wish to put a question. This he must do through the judge.

When the testimony has been completed, the whole deposition is read back to the witness. At this stage, he may wish to correct, alter, or even remove some or all the answers already given, and he is permitted to do so. When the deposition has been corrected, all those present sign the testimony. At this point, the witness may be asked to take a further oath. By this second oath he confirms that the statements made in the deposition are true, and he also swears that he will not disclose the questions asked nor the replies given until the end of the case. This additional oath is not usually asked of solicitors or other professional men such as doctors since in any case they are bound by their own code of professional etiquette.

The purpose of the oath of secrecy is this: in a canonical court there is no power of subpoena, nor can there be any public penalty for perjury. Moreover, since the process is obviously secret—the intimate details of a person's private life must clearly remain secret—it is also necessary to safeguard the proceedings against the subornation of witnesses. To some extent the oath of secrecy, to last until the proceedings have been completed, safeguards the petitioner from later accusations of his witnesses having been 'briefed'. However, most judges find by experience that even when one of the witnesses lies under oath, the truth ultimately emerges in some way.

The session may have lasted—in a complicated matter—for some three or four hours. Indeed sometimes it might be necessary for the petitioner to come back again for a further session to complete the testimony. But since the petitioner appreciates that this is for his own good, there is rarely any objection to this. For other witnesses, the evidence sessions are usually shorter. However, judges find that to hurry these sessions is useless, since the difficulty for a person searching his recollections—sometimes ten or more years back—is immense. An attempt to hurry the witness is not helpful.

Subsequently, the evidence of the respondent and the other witnesses is taken. Normally, for a formal evidence session, the same persons as mentioned above are present. Depending upon the complexity of the case there may be as many as six or even more witnesses to be heard. Frequently, some of the witnesses live a long way from the tribunal offices; sometimes they live abroad. But it is usually quite easy to obtain this testimony. A request is sent to the dioceses where the other witnesses live. The local tribunals take the required testimony, with the same formalities as mentioned above. The testimony thus taken is returned to the court and included in the dossier of the case. In this way it is possible to obtain evidence from places as far apart as South America and Australia, and even from otherwise almost inaccessible places such as Poland and Hungary. Wherever the Church has a tribunal, it is possible to obtain the required testimony.

When all the evidence originally requested by the advocate and the 'defender of the bond' has been taken, and transcribed (usually in five copies—three for the judges, and one each for the defender and advocate), it is then 'published'. That is to say the whole of the dossier is made available to the advocate and the 'defender of the bond' to study. Both of them carefully study the dossier. At this point, the defender and the advocate have the opportunity of calling for more witnesses, even, for good reasons, for the re-interrogation of certain witnesses. For example, it may become clear that the testimony given by some of the early witnesses has not dealt with a point that only came to light towards the end. It would be reasonable to have certain of the witnesses re-interrogated on this point. However, to call further witnesses or to have a witness re-interrogated may only be done through and with the permission of the presiding judge.

When both defender and advocate are satisfied that all the possible and relevant testimony has been obtained, the presiding judge then declares the evidence stage of the case 'concluded'. At this point, the advocate is requested to prepare his pleadings showing why, from the evidence, the marriage in question should be regarded as null and void. He is given a certain length of time to write his observations, and within this time he must send them to the presiding judge. A copy of the pleadings are also supplied to the 'defender of the bond', who then prepares his reply to the advocate. The defender shows, again from the evidence, why the marriage should be regarded as valid. The advocate and defender have the opportunity of writing two (and, sometimes in very complicated cases, three) sets of comments. Thereafter, the presiding judge declares this stage completed.

Copies of all the evidence, documents and the submissions of advocate and defender are then handed to the three judges in the case. A certain length of time is given for the judges to study the material, and a date is set for them to meet and discuss the case. Before the meeting, however, each of the judges has independently reached his own conclusion on the case, and he comes to the meeting with a few pages of reasons showing why he has reached his decision. At this meeting, called the *decisio*, the presiding judge calls upon the *ponens* to expound the facts of the case and the judges discuss their views. It is open to the judges to change their minds during the meeting. When the discussion is concluded, there is a vote and the result of the case rests upon the majority decision. The formula of the decision would be expressed, for example, thus: 'It appears proved (not proved) that the marriage in question is null and void on the grounds of an intention against the permanence of the marriage on the part of the respondent'.

Where there is a negative decision, it will be noticed that the judges make no comment on the validity of the marriage as such. The decision merely states that 'it appears to be unproved'. Thus when there is a negative decision given against the petitioner and judges are merely stating that the petitioner has not proved the invalidity. This is an important point, since it is always possible that the judges may have concluded that there is insufficient evidence to establish the nullity, whereas if there had been evidence, the marriage might well have been proved to be null and void. Hence, any comment on the *validity* of a marriage is carefully avoided.

The outcome of the meeting is advised to the petitioner and his advocate, and the defender, at once. It is then the obligation of the *ponens* to write the *sentence*. This is a series of reasons in law and in fact showing why and how the judges arrived at their decision. It sets out briefly a short synopsis of the case, then it gives the relevant points of the law as they apply to the case in hand, and finally follow a series of arguments of the law applied to the alleged facts, showing the reasons for the decision. When the sentence has been produced (some weeks after the decision) this is also released to the petitioner and his advocate, and to the defender.

If the decision is in favour of the petitioner—i.e. the judges have decided that the marriage is invalid—the 'defender of the bond' is bound, according to the present general law, to appeal against the decision. On the other hand, if the decision is against the petitioner, the latter has the right to appeal against it. In either case, the petition and all evidence of the 'first instance' (the court that tried it first) must go on appeal to a 'court of second instance'.

The procedure for the appeal from an affirmative decision is regulated by special provisions of the Holy See[1]. There are two possible methods of procedure for a case heard by the appeal court. The first and shortest way is by means of *ratification;* the other way is termed the *ordinary procedure.* When a case is received by the appeal court, a defender of the bond is appointed to examine all the evidence and other documents. The defender then prepares a report on the case indicating whether he thinks that there would be no problems—and he would have no objection—if the appeal court judges confirm the first instance affirmative decision; that is give it a further affirmative and issue a decree of nullity. On the other hand he may feel there are special problems which have not been adequately dealt with by the first instance court, and these problems should receive further attention from the appeal court.

The judges then consider the case. If they conclude that the case is indeed straightforward, and the decision of the first instance court is correct, they can proceed to *ratify* that first instance decision; and issue a decree of nullity. On the other hand, they may feel that the case requires further work, and therefore they issue a decree directing that the case should be dealt with by the *ordinary procedure,* and they give reasons for this direction. The advocate may in such circumstances think that more evidence is needed and calls for this, either of someone who has already given testimony, or from someone new. In any event, whatever further work is necessary on the case is attended to; and thereafter the advocate and

---

[1] *Motu proprio* of Paul VI: *Causas Matrimoniales* of 27 March 1971.

the defender write their comments, as already explained for the first instance procedure. The judges then consider the case, discuss and decide it; with the duly appointed *ponens* writing the reasons in law and fact for the decision.

In any event for there to be issued a decree of nullity it is already clear that there must be two *concordant* or agreeing decisions in favour of the petition. If one decision is affirmative and the other negative, before a decree can be issued the case must be examined by a third court[1]. Below we will deal with the Sacred Roman Rota which often plays the part of a third instance court; although there are other means by which a case can receive a third hearing without reference to Rome. This will also be mentioned.

There is one further point, however, that needs a mention. It will be evident from some of the grounds of nullity already mentioned that where a case is proved and the grounds reside in the petitioner, it may be necessary to exercise some considerable caution about this petitioner marrying again. For example, in the case where a non-Catholic petitioner alleged that he had an intention against the permanence of marriage when entering his first union, this intention *contra bonum sacramenti,* as it is called, is proved to have existed. It is a matter of ordinary prudence to make quite certain that when this non-Catholic marries again this time in the Catholic Church, he does not have an intention of a similar nature. Consequently to make quite sure that his intentions are proper this time it is not unusual for the appeal court to add a restrictive or an *ad mentem* clause to the decree of nullity. This clause would say something to the effect that the "petitioner should not be permitted to enter into a new marriage in the Catholic Church until such time as he has satisfied the bishop of the place where he lives that he now has a proper intention with regard to the permanence of marriage". As a result of such a clause, the petitioner would probably be asked to sign a specially drafted document making clear that his intentions this time are right; and also the bishop might require that the circumstances of the nullity of the first union are explained to the new fiancée.

The situation can sometimes be complicated by the decree of nullity being given in a case where the lack of due discretion or *amentia* or the inability to assume the obligations of marriage were alleged (and proved). In these circumstances it may be necessary to place an *absolute* bar upon a person remarrying—for example, if the person in question is still in the same state as he was at the time of the first union. This would manifestly be the case with *amentia ;* and

---

[1]  An appeal from a negative decision given in first instance is dealt with according to the ordinary procedure.

this would also often be the reason why a person who wishes to petition on the basis of his own *amentia* would probably be excluded from bringing the case; since there is a fair chance that if the grounds were proved that person would still be suffering from the same condition. This is of course not always the situation; but it will be appreciated that great caution has to be paid to situations when something of this sort might occur.

The above account is a very brief outline of the formal nullity procedure. It will have been clear from this that certain basic elements underlie the procedure. We have already mentioned the matter of the type or nature of the process, that it is not like the English civil law process but essentially a documentary and closed procedure. There are a number of other points, which must now be mentioned. In these notes we will deal with the burden of proof, the possibility of rejection of a petition at the very outset, the part played in the nullity procedure by the Sacred Roman Rota, and the matter of the time and the expenses involved.

THE BURDEN OF PROOF

In any legal process there must be certain assumptions upon which the court may rest. For example, in civil law there is a presumption that the ordinary man knows what he is doing when he performs some action. It is not *assumed* that the person concerned is mentally unbalanced—this must be proved. Again when a person buys a suite of furniture, it is assumed that he actually intends to do this. Subsequently he may seek to prove that at the time he was not mentally competent or some other fact that would mean the contract was invalid. In Canon Law, it is assumed that when a person says the words and performs certain actions at the altar during the wedding ceremony, he intends to convey by these means some interior disposition by which he intends to get married. Thus when a person has made the answers and indicated his consent to the marriage, he is presumed to have intended to marry.

If, subsequently, he or his partner wishes to impugn the validity of the marriage—for example, to assert that the man did not have the intention to contract marriage at all—then it would be for the person making this allegation to prove it. This is obvious and reasonable. Hence, when we speak of the burden of proof in connection with a nullity case we mean that the onus of establishing that the marriage is invalid (i.e. that the person did not intend to contract the marriage) lies upon the person alleging this—that is, upon the petitioner. It follows from this that the petitioner must bring forward such evidence as will upset the presumption that the man concerned intended to contract a proper marriage. In other words, there is a presumption that a marriage is valid, which remains until this presumption is upset. This is the task of the petitioner. When the petitioner is not successful in bringing forward sufficient evidence to upset the presumption of validity, the judges must return a decision of *non constat de nullitate* or 'it does not appear that the marriage in question is invalid'.

### THE REJECTION OF THE PETITION

We have already mentioned that there is a stage, just after the appointment of the court, when the petition submitted is examined and if it does not conform to the rules of competence or it it does not have some substance as a case, it is rejected. That is to say the court rules that the petition cannot be tried. When rejecting a petition, the court must give reasons for the rejection. There are two principal reasons: one relating to competence, and the other relating to lack of substance or at least that the petition does not state adequately the substance which may well exist. If the rejection is on the grounds that the tribunal is not competent to deal with the case, the petitioner must be advised of this, and also told which would be the competent tribunal to whom the petition should be submitted. On the other hand, if the petition is not evidently based upon adequate grounds of nullity this must also be indicated to the petitioner. It may happen that the petition has been badly drawn up and that it does not express what is in the petitioner's mind, in which case it might be possible for the person concerned to alter the petition, and provide further details which would make it acceptable to the court.

But it can also happen that the court rejects the petition on the basis that there is insufficient substance to the case—that is to say either that even if proved the grounds alleged would not indicate the nullity of marriage, or else that the grounds alleged are patently false. A court might also reject a petition if it is quite clear that, though there are *grounds* for nullity, it is evidently impossible to establish these grounds through the necessary evidence. In any event, if the petition is rejected and cannot be altered by the petitioner, the latter has the right of appeal against the rejection. This appeal is made to the usual appeal court appointed for the diocese. On appeal, a court is appointed, and three judges consider the petition. If they regard the rejection by the first instance court as unjustified, they direct the first instance tribunal to take and try the case. In these circumstances, a new panel of judges is appointed for the trial of the case in the original court. Thus the judges who first of all rejected the petition are not members of the court who actually try the petition at the direction of the court of second instance.

There is another circumstance which must be considered at this point in connection with a petition being rejected. It may occur that the petitioner was himself the cause of the alleged nullity. For example, the petitioner may have wilfully prepared documents before the marriage to show that he did not intend to contract a permanent union, and now having tired of his wife, he produces these documents to show that his marriage is invalid. It may indeed be true that the marriage is invalid for the reason stated. However, since the person concerned was also the malicious cause of the nullity, he is barred from petitioning. This is obviously a very proper provision of the law, otherwise unscrupulous persons would be the cause of turning the marriage bond into a farce. On the other hand, if the innocent (and this must be shown) spouse chooses to petition, the court would certainly accept her claim to a trial of the marriage.

### THE PART PLAYED BY THE SACRED ROMAN ROTA

It will be clear from the account of the nullity process already given that in normal circumstances the Sacred Roman Rota is not involved in the ordinary diocesan trial of marriage cases. But there are situations in which the Rota may be involved. We have already mentioned the necessity of there being two affirmative decisions before a decree of nullity can be issued. Where the petitioner has received one affirmative and one negative decision, a third hearing is required. The case can be sent to the Sacred Roman Rota to be dealt with in the third instance. An affirmative decision given then would mean that a decree of nullity could be granted. However it is not always necessary to go to the Rota for a third hearing of a case. The Holy See does give permission—though on an *ad hoc* basis—for a third hearing to take place in some diocese locally. The advantage of this procedure—of a third instance hearing dealt with locally—is speed. The Rota has a large number of cases, and the procedure there is consequently slower than when dealt with locally.

Another situation in which a case might be referred to the Rota is when the petitioner, having received a negative decision in first instance wishes to appeal directly (in second instance) to the Rota. This he is permitted to do; but it then means that if the second decision is affirmative, the third instance hearing must also be dealt with at the Rota (with another panel of judges). Moreover for very special reasons a person may request to have his case dealt with from the very beginning by the Rota. This may happen when, for example, the petitioner is very well known in his own diocese and by the members of the tribunal there. He can be given permission to start his case from the beginning with the Rota.

TIME AND EXPENSE

It will have been noticed that the procedure described, because of the great care taken with the processing of a nullity case, must involve a very considerable time. The actual amount of time taken in the treatment of a case depends largely on the tribunal concerned. Obviously where the tribunal is small, where there are not many cases, the personnel will be relatively inexperienced in the actual processing of the cases that do come before them. This could mean very considerable delay. On the other hand, where there is a much larger tribunal dealing with a much larger volume of cases, though the processing of a case may take a shorter time, the expenses will be, for that very reason, much heavier. It is clear that the time factor or the expenses involved cannot be analysed here since these depend largely on the tribunal concerned. The petitioner would be wise to obtain an idea of how long the case will take by asking the officials of the tribunal, where also some indication of the expenses involved will be discovered[1].

At the moment, there are moves being made in many countries to reduce the delays that can ensue in nullity cases. Probably the principal means of reducing the delays and the difficulties involved is by the introduction of regional courts. This means gathering several diocesan tribunals together into one unit thereby having larger units, but a smaller number of them, in a country. The results of such regionalisation have already shown the merits of the system.

## NOTE ON THE INFORMAL OR ADMINISTRATIVE PROCEDURE

We have already indicated that there is one procedure for the treatment of nullity cases which involve some sort of defect of consent, and that this same procedure is also used for the proof of certain diriment impediments. However, there are other impediments, though causing the nullity of the marriage, which can be established by means of an informal procedure. This informal procedure demands that the impediment itself should be established by means of *certain* and *authentic documents*. If such documents can be produced, then together with the citations mentioned in connection with the formal procedure, and the inspection of the documents by the 'defender of the bond', such a marriage can be declared invalid without further ado. To illustrate

---

[1]   The expenses of a case can vary considerably; in large diocesan or regional tribunals, they may be between £100 and £150. However, where the petitioner is unable to afford these costs, special arrangements can be made for ecclesiastical 'legal aid' by which the person agrees to contribute towards part of the expenses, or in some cases have all the expenses remitted.

the working of this procedure, we give below a short case together with what information must be obtained to demonstrate the nullity of the marriage. Before turning to the example, however, we must recall that the informal process can be used for establishing the following impediments: disparity of cult, a solemn vow of chastity, sacred orders, previous marriage, consanguinity, affinity and spiritual relationship.

*Example of an informal case for the impediment of previous marriage*

Peter Smith speaks to his parish priest about getting married, and tells him that he is in love with Doreen who was previously married. He tells the priest that since Doreen had been married in the register office, he had always assumed that this was an invalid marriage, and that, therefore, at some time he would be able to marry her. The priest warns Peter that, assuming Doreen is not a Catholic, and assuming that Doreen's former husband was not a Catholic either, her marriage is very probably valid. However, the priest says that he will go into the case, take some details and refer Peter to the local tribunal. The priest sees Doreen and discovers that neither Doreen nor her husband were Catholics. But he does learn that Doreen's former husband had been previously married and divorced. The priest, thereupon, refers Peter and Doreen to the tribunal.

When Doreen is interviewed at the tribunal, the following story emerges. Doreen had been married to James Williamson on 14th April 1961, but James had left Doreen for another woman, and Doreen had divorced James. The decree of divorce was made absolute on 19th March 1966. Doreen knew that James had been married previously but she did not know much about this union; and nothing about the former wife other than that James had always called her an agnostic. James had divorced her on the grounds of adultery. Doreen did not have anything else to tell the tribunal.

The *officialis* instructs Doreen to obtain from the General Register Office a copy of her marriage certificate relating to the union with James. This certificate shows that James had been formerly married. Therefore, a search is made for certificates relating to a marriage and a divorce in the name of James Williamson prior to April 1961. After some searching the documents were discovered. They show that James Williamson had married Sandra Hope on 18th November 1956, and that James was described as single as also was Sandra. A divorce decree also found shows that this same union had been dissolved, and the decree had been made absolute on 16th July 1960. The *officialis* also asks Doreen to make a further search for a marriage certificate in the name of Sandra Hope or Sandra Williamson for sometime after July 1960. Such a certificate is found, and it shows that Sandra had been remarried on 24th July 1961 to a man named Cyril Peterson. Finally, the *officialis* asks Doreen to find out something about the religion of James and Sandra. Doreen knows James's mother, and the latter is able to state that James had been baptized in the Church of England in a certain village in Norfolk. From there, Doreen obtains a copy of James's baptismal certificate. James's mother also knew that Sandra was an unbeliever and that her parents had also been unbelievers. She knew that Sandra's mother had originally been a member, though a non-practising one, of the Presbyterian Church, but Sandra had never been raised in any religion at all.

When all this information had been established, the *officialis* makes a list of all the documents that he has obtained, and alongside each document he shows what the document establishes. The following are the documents that had been produced:

1. Marriage certificate of James Williamson and Sandra Hope, married on 18th November 1956 at the Chiswick Register Office.
2. Divorce decree absolute for the same union; made absolute on 16th July 1960.
3. Baptismal certificate of James Williamson (Church of England), and testimony of James's mother that he had always belonged to the Church of England.
4. Information from James's mother—on oath—that Sandra Hope had been the child of non-Catholic parents; and brought up with little or no religion.
5. Marriage certificate of Sandra Williamson and Cyril Peterson, married on 24th July 1961 at Chelsea Register Office.
6. Marriage certificate of James Williamson and Doreen, married on 14th April 1961 at the Paddington Register Office.
7. Divorce decree absolute for the same union (i.e. no. 6 above); made absolute on 19th March 1966.

With all this information, the *officialis* can make out a statement that when James had married Doreen he was already, in terms of Canon Law, married to Sandra. To all intents and purposes the union with Sandra had been valid—neither were bound to the form of marriage (since neither were Catholics), and both were at the time of this first marriage single persons. Furthermore, when James married Doreen Sandra was still alive (as shown by the fact that she contracted a marriage after the date of Doreen's marriage to James). Hence, when all the documents have been produced, and James has been cited (i.e. advised that his marriage to Doreen was undergoing scrutiny with a view to an ecclesiastical declaration of nullity, and advised of the reasons), the 'defender of the bond' is able to examine and state that all the documents are in order. Thereafter, the *officialis* submits the documents to the bishop, who signs the declaration of nullity.

This is a short example of the informal process for nullity, which, together with the other (formal) process, are the ones used by the Church either when it is alleged that there was something wrong with the consent of one of the parties, or when there was an alleged undispensed diriment impediment preventing a couple from marrying validly. We now leave our consideration of the nullity of marriage and turn to the Church's procedure for dispensing a marriage that has not been consummated.

# Chapter 7

## DISPENSATION OF AN UNCONSUMMATED MARRIAGE

We have already said that according to the teaching of the Church a marriage which is valid, sacramental and consummated cannot be set aside by any human power. Such a union is regarded as indissoluble, binding until the death of one of the spouses. In the preceding chapters we have examined the situation if it is alleged that a marriage is not valid. In this chapter we look at the situation, and the possibilities, if the marriage is alleged to be unconsummated. First of all it should be said that the teaching that the Pope has the power to dispense a marriage which has never been consummated goes back to the Middle Ages. There was considerable discussion amongst theologians and lawyers concerning precisely what constituted marriage. It will be appreciated that the view which maintained that the marriage was made, or came into being, through consummation, was also implicitly stating that until consummation had taken place, the marriage had not yet fully come into being. On the other hand, the view which maintained that consent made the marriage, was not disregarding the elements of consummation altogether. But it did not regard consummation as being the constitutive element of marriage; though without consummation it was hardly a complete marriage.

Apart from the historical aspect of the matter, it is quite clear when speaking of marriage as a union in which the parties pledge to each other the rights over their bodies, where consummation does not take place, there is something missing from the fulfilment of this pledge. When a couple marry validly, but agree that they will not make use of their marital rights, this very statement indicates that they do appreciate that they have exchanged these marital rights. However, when a couple do choose to exercise their marital rights, but for some reason, other than their own wills, this exercise cannot take place, then there is something deficient in their marriage. When this deficiency is caused by the will of one of the parties, obviously the other party is gravely wronged, even on the basis of a natural contract, let alone on the basis of a sacramental union. Thus when a marriage has not been consummated (unless it is by the express and free agreement of both parties), then there is something gravely amiss with the union. It is this type of union with which we will now deal.

There are a few types of tribunal case which carry with them the pain and suffering involved in a marriage that has failed through the tension arising from sexual troubles between a couple. Since the sexual life of the parties is a normal and holy part of marriage involving the participation with God in the possible formation and creation of a new human being, and which is the normal and expected means through which a couple will show their love one for the other, the failure in this respect usually produces a state almost amounting to shock—certainly of frustration, sometimes of anger, and always a deep unhappiness on the part of at least one of the spouses. This is often an area of marriage in which the couple are too shy to seek advice. Often they merely hope and pray that something will happen so that all will come right. Unfortunately, because of this tendency to say little and to remain silent about the problem, sometimes the trouble is allowed to persist too long, and by the time help is sought it may be too late.

The work of the Catholic Marriage Advisory Council is much centred in this area of marriage problems. However by the time the couple have referred to this or similar organizations, it may be too late. The marriage may have broken down, or at the very least the health of one or both of the parties may have suffered so considerably as a result of the problem that there is sometimes little else a couple can do but separate. It is quite obvious, therefore, that wherever a problem such as this arises in a marriage—normally very soon after the marriage—help should be sought at once. The work of marriage tribunals is sad, since they so frequently have to deal with marriages that have already broken down for this reason.

It is frequently said, since the couple when they marry agree that they will pledge themselves to each other 'in sickness and in health', that merely because a couple have not been able to have intercourse, this is hardly a reason for separating. This is to misunderstand the nature of marriage, and to over-estimate the human condition. Where the couple have pledged themselves to each other for life— including the physical rights over their bodies—there is an assumption that normal intercourse will be able to take place. This assumption is based on the whole notion of the mutual physical exchange. If it is not possible for this exchange to be fulfilled, there is obviously something missing from the union. Even though the condition in one of the parties may be the result of some sickness, nonetheless the words 'in sickness and in health' hardly refer to this type of sickness, which strikes at the whole basis of the marriage. It is for this reason that for certain special situations and upon certain conditions, the Holy Father sometimes grants a dispensation, which enables one or both parties to remarry.

In a non-consummation case put to the Holy Father, there are two elements that must be clearly established. One element is that the marriage has not in fact been consummated, and the other is that there are sufficiently good reasons why the dispensation should be granted. We will now deal with these two requirements.

## PROOF OF NON-CONSUMMATION

To begin with, it is necessary that we state clearly what the Church understands by consummation. The age old definition of consummation is: the penetration of the vagina by the erect male member, and the depositing of true semen within the vagina. We have already seen something of the present matter when dealing with the impediment of impotence. Obviously, for consummation to take place, the definition mentioned above must be fulfilled. Rather than deal here with physical conditions which prevent consummation—which would come under the heading of impotence—we will concentrate upon proof of *the fact* that the marriage has not been consummated. It is necessary to appreciate that wherever there exists a condition of absolute or relative impotence which is perpetual, and antecedent to the marriage, then obviously the marriage will be impossible of consummation. However, here we will deal with the situation—which all too frequently arises—where separately, all the elements of the definition above seem to be possible, but for some other reason the marriage is not consummated. For example, it might be possible for there to be proper and complete erection of the male member, and yet still be no consummation, in the canonical sense. Or though the male is capable of erection and ejaculation he may not be capable of penetration.

Frequently, medical specialists advise that there is no evident bar to consummation, and yet nonetheless it has not taken place. This can often be due to a lack of confidence on the part of the couple, or nervousness, or fear, with consequent tension preventing penetration. It is well to remember that, generally, non-consummation is the fault of neither spouse, and often with different partners consummation may be a matter of ease and simplicity. However, the task of the matrimonial tribunal is to collect the evidence and try to establish the facts.

Since the dispensation of marriage—even on the grounds of non-consummation—is a power only exercised by the Holy Father himself, the first point to be stated here is that local diocesan tribunals act as agents for the Holy See. They do not act 'of their own proper competence', and the final decision in the case is taken in Rome, not by the local tribunal. When the dossier has been completed by the local tribunal it is submitted to the Congregation of the Sacraments in Rome.

To begin a non-consummation case, it is necessary to have various documents and a petition. The documents are the baptismal and marriage certificates, proof that the marriage has broken down (e.g. civil divorce or nullity decree). With these documents the bishop is then able to appoint a court to take the evidence in the case.

For this type of case the court consists of an 'instructing judge', the 'defender of the bond', and a notary. The instructing judge arranges for the petitioner to give evidence. It is assumed—for the purposes of this description of the process—that the petitioner has already been examined by a doctor (who, it is hoped, may have been able to certify that the girl is a *virgo intacta*). However it is not the situation that without a medical report a case can never be sent to Rome. It depends on the case.

Since, as it will be appreciated, some of the evidence that must be taken is of a very personal nature, it is helpful if the interrogation of the wife be carried out by a doctor. Hence those questions which deal with the actual details of attempts at consummation and the like would often be dealt with by the doctor appointed by the court. This interrogation by the doctor may be carried out in a hospital or in the doctor's consulting rooms or at the tribunal. Besides the questions by the doctor, the petitioner is also asked by the instructing judge (on the same or some other occasions) questions on more general matters; e.g. how she came to meet her husband, when they married, whether they were happy to begin with, how and when the marriage started to break down. Where possible the instructing judge would be accompanied by a notary. When all this evidence has been taken down, it is checked through by the petitioner and signed. There is also here an oath of secrecy to be taken by all the witnesses. The members of the court are already bound by their strict oath of office, and the doctor is in any case bound by his bond of professional confidence. Thereafter, the evidence of the other spouse is taken.

The very nature of this type of case is such that there can be no witnesses in the strict sense of the word. Indeed it will have been observed that this type of case goes through—apart from the evidence of the doctors—entirely upon the word and good standing and known honesty of the two parties to the case as verified by the witnesses. However, it will be seen that the term 'witness' covers

two different kinds of person. There is one type of witness who
states what he knows about consummation of the marriage. That is,
he says what he has 'heard' about this. In this sense he is a hearsay
witness, but provided that the evidence can be assessed as truthful
and relevant, such hearsay witnesses can be very valuable for the
establishment of the truth. The other type of witness is a 'character'
witness. That is, since the case is based very much upon the
truthfulness and good faith of the parties, it is necessary to have the
statements of witnesses who can vouch for the truthfulness and
honesty of the parties. The court will try to assemble—from the two
parties—the names and addresses of both hearsay and character
witnesses.

We can show here by means of an example how the testimony of
these two types of witness can be of assistance. Let us call the
petitioner Sophie, and her husband Robert. They had met at their
Teachers Training College. They married in 1963, and although
they attempted intercourse on many occasions, this was never
successful. After about a year—during which time they had
mentioned the trouble to no one—they realised they must seek help
and they saw their general practitioner. He examined them both but
he could find nothing physically wrong with either party. Thinking
that the trouble might be psychological, he referred them to a
Catholic psychiatrist. The latter realised that there was something
radically wrong with Robert, and began treatment. In the
meanwhile, Sophie confided her troubles to her mother, who also
mentioned the matter to her husband. The mother, feeling unable
to be of any real assistance, also suggested that Sophie should speak
to her older sister, who was happily married with four children.
Sophie, therefore, confided in the sister, Veronica.

Unfortunately, the treatment that Robert received did not help,
and indeed matters became steadily worse. The effect on the nerves
of both Sophie and Robert was appalling. Finally the psychiatrist,
realizing that he could not help Robert, suggested that for the sake
of the couple's health, they might try a temporary separation. Being
ready to try any remedy, the couple separated. They both still felt
they were very much in love, but that the strain of the relationship
was corroding their lives. When they did come together again, there
was still no improvement. By this time the general practitioner was
becoming alarmed about the effect on Sophie, and he consulted with
the psychiatrist. They both thought that the only remedy to the sad
situation was for the couple to separate again, with the option of
returning to each other in three months. However, after the three
months had elapsed, Sophie was no better, and it was thought that
permanent separation was the only solution. Both Sophie and

Robert realized that there was no hope for them together, and so they parted in mid-1965.

Sophie slowly returned to health after her near nervous breakdown. Robert also recovered, but the couple could not go back to each other. Sophie approached the tribunal to see whether the Holy Father would grant a dispensation, so that she could remarry and have children. Robert was also anxious to remarry and to have children too, and he readily agreed that this approach to the Holy Father was the proper course.

The tribunal, having considered this a worthy petition, begins a non-consummation case. Sophie gives her evidence, being questioned about the intimate side of the married life by a tribunal doctor. She had already been examined by one doctor, and his report stated that Sophie was a *virgo intacta*. Thereafter, Robert gives evidence to the court. Meanwhile, the tribunal compiles a list of those who could give evidence in the case. Firstly, there is the petitioner's mother and father, and the sister Veronica. Robert had also mentioned the matter to his father at the time that he first began to receive treatment from the psychiatrist. Two other witnesses are the general practitioner and the psychiatrist. The two doctors, being bound by their bond of professional confidence, may only answer questions for the tribunal, provided their respective patients sign release notes. The couple give these releases. Besides the persons already mentioned, the instructing judge obtains the names of three persons, able to state that they know Sophie well, and can vouch for her truthfulness. These are her parish priest, the headmistress of the school where she was a pupil, and the director of the Teachers Training College where she trained as a teacher for three years before the marriage. Robert suggests the names of three 'character' witnesses for himself. They are: a priest, with whom he trained at College; his present assistant headmaster (of the school where he teaches); and a great friend of his own family who has known Robert since childhood and has kept in close touch with him after leaving school.

All these persons are asked to give 'evidence' to the tribunal[1]. The 'hearsay' witnesses are asked, amongst other things, when they were first told about the couple's marriage problem, whether this was before or after the separation, and any other relevant details they might know about. The 'character' witnesses are asked about the honesty and truthfulness of the parties. When all this material has been gathered, it is transcribed into four copies. One of these copies

---

[1]   It should be stated that cases have, however, been submitted to Rome with much less evidence than was gathered in this case.

is sent to the 'defender of the bond' who was probably present at most of the evidence sessions. He carefully examines all the evidence, and sees whether it contains any inherent contradictions. He sees to what extent the spouses are vouched for as honest and trustworthy, and makes certain that, so far as is possible, all the regulations of the Sacred Congregation of the Sacraments on this matter have been observed. Any observations that he has to make on either of these two counts he sets down in his 'comments' which he returns to the tribunal.

The whole dossier together with the comments of the 'defender of the bond' are then submitted to the bishop. Often the instructing judge has been through all the material himself and made some comments for the assistance of the bishop. In any event the bishop prepares his 'opinion' on the case, specially mentioning whether he regards the allegation of non-consummation as established, whether the petitioner is a worthy person, and whether he recommends the petition to the Holy Father. This 'opinion', together with three copies of the whole dossier, is then sent to the Congregation of the Sacraments in Rome.

At the Congregation, where the case is handled on behalf of the Holy Father, another court is appointed. This time, the court consists of a 'defender of the bond' and three commissioners. The 'defender of the bond' examines the case, and writes his comments. He passes these to the Congregation, and the comments together with the whole dossier are then submitted to each of the three commissioners. These priests carefully and independently examine all the material, and at some appointed time they meet and vote on the case. If the decision is in favour of the petition (i.e. if they decide that the evidence has established the non-consummation and a dispensation should be granted), their recommendations are then submitted to the Cardinal Prefect of the Congregation. The latter personally takes a resumé of this case, together with many others, to the Holy Father and advises him of the opinion of the Sacred Congregation. If the Holy Father agrees, the Congregation then issues the necessary dispensation in the name of the Pope. In due course this decree will be sent to the local diocese, and the instructing judge will communicate the decision to the parties concerned. On receipt of the dispensation, provided there are no restrictive clauses inserted in the text, both parties are advised that they are now free to remarry.

Having dealt with the procedure for handling a case, we must now consider a few further points, namely the merits of the petitioner, restrictive clauses and the time and expenses involved in a non-consummation case.

THE MERITS OF THE PETITIONER

As we have already mentioned, since we are speaking of a valid and sacramental union, a dispensation of an unconsummated marriage is something granted by the Holy Father as a favour and not as a right. For this reason, the merits of the petitioner and the reasons for the petition will be carefully considered in deciding whether to grant the dispensation, once the non-consummation has been established. Firstly, under this heading it must be mentioned that the Holy See will not accept a petition when there has been a history of contraception in the marriage. It will be appreciated that where use has been made of sheath contraceptives (i.e. those which are sound) and this was the only form of intercourse, it follows that according to the definition already given, consummation in the strict sense may not have taken place. In such circumstances, a person could technically allege that his marriage has not been consummated. However, the Holy See does not accept a petition where this has been the case. One reason is that since this is a favour granted where the couple have not been able to have intercourse, it would be too much of a fiction if the Holy See granted a dispensation where the contravention of the Church's law has been made the basis of the petition. The other reason, equally important, is that since it is never certain, and obviously not capable of proof, that a sheath contraceptive is effective, it cannot be stated with certainty that semen has never been deposited in the vagina. Obviously in the case of other contraceptive devices, or of the pill, this latter point does not arise since the definition of consummation is either realized or it is not.

Besides this point, the Holy See always seeks a reason for granting a dispensation, even when it has been established with moral certainty that a marriage has not been consummated. Therefore, merely to petition the Holy See so as to contract another marriage where the person concerned has been the *wilful* cause of the breakdown of the first union would not be considered as a reason for granting the dispensation. However, since anyone petitioning the Holy See for this favour obviously has a reason—normally to remarry within the Church, to have a family and to lead a normal Catholic family life—this point is usually academic. It is merely mentioned here in order to stress that the granting of the dispensation does not automatically follow upon proof of non-consummation.

RESTRICTIVE CLAUSES

Occasionally the reason for the non-consummation may be the antecedent and perpetual impotence of one of the parties. Or rather, it might be surmised that this is the reason. Or the reason may be that one of the parties was the deliberate and wilful cause of the non-consummation—i.e. the person concerned refused to consummate the marriage. When the Holy Father grants a dispensation, it means that the marriage in question is dissolved. Thus, at least technically, both parties are free to contract other marriages. Even the guilty party could be free to marry again. It is for this reason that occasionally the Holy See imposes a restrictive clause on the dispensation. It might be stated, for example, that the other party is not to be permitted to remarry without the permission of the Bishop of the diocese, or of the Sacred Congregation; or, indeed, that the other party is not to be permitted to remarry at all.

The reason for such restrictive clauses will readily be appreciated. However, it will be asked how this restriction can be made to apply where the other party—the restricted one—may move to another place where he is not known, and where none of the local clergy are aware of the previous marriage. The way it operates is this. Whenever a person seeks to marry in the Church, it is necessary for him to produce amongst other documents, a baptismal certificate dated within six months of the marriage to be contracted. This is one of the essential documents in every marriage dossier. When the marriage has taken place, the priest sends a notification concerning the details of the marriage to the places of the baptism of the two parties. An entry concerning the marriage is made in the Baptismal Register. In the same way when a dispensation is granted because a marriage has not been consummated, a note of this fact is also recorded in the Baptismal and Marriage Registers. If there is a restrictive clause attached to the dispensation this too is entered with the Baptismal Register. When a person wants to remarry, he must obtain a recent copy of his baptismal certificate, and this copy will mention the restrictive clause. In this way, proper control over marriages taking place in the Church can be exercised.

TIME AND EXPENSE

As we mentioned in connection with the nullity procedure, the time and expense of a non-consummation case depends on a number of factors. The size of the tribunal will determine more often than not how speedily a case is dealt with. If it is a large tribunal with a number of such cases being handled, then it is likely that a non-consummation petition will be dealt with more speedily, through the very familiarity that those working in a large tribunal have with this type of case. Where the tribunal is large, however, the expenses are likely to be greater. On the other hand, where the tribunal is smaller then the costs may be lower, but the speed factor may be affected[1]. Hence, it is not possible to establish a rule about how long such cases will take to be prepared in the local diocese. But since all such cases must go to Rome, it is possible for the tribunal to calculate the average time taken in Rome, so the local tribunal will probably be able to advise the petitioner how long his case may take with the Congregation of Sacraments.

In this chapter we have tried to describe the typical procedure for a non-consummation case. Naturally there will be considerable variation in the details depending upon who the petitioner is, i.e. husband or wife; depending upon whether both parties co-operate; whether there is adequate evidence of the facts alleged, and many other factors. Here we have merely outlined the simplest type of non-consummation case, and obviously this outline cannot cover all the possible combinations of circumstances. However, the description of the procedure will convey some idea of the work involved in such a case. We must now proceed to examine the other type of case involving the setting aside of marriage, namely, the 'privilege of the faith' case.

---

[1]  The point concerning ecclesiastical legal aid applies here to the expenses of a non-consummation case as it did in a nullity case.

## Chapter 8

# DISSOLUTION OF THE NATURAL BOND

We have already explained what the Church understands as grounds for invalidity of marriage, and also what is understood by the non-consummation of a union. Finally, we must deal with the situation when it is alleged that the marriage contracted is not a sacrament. When we speak of a marriage being non-sacramental, we have to bear in mind that the sacrament of marriage, like the other sacraments, can only be received by a person who is himself a Christian. Moreover since the sacrament of matrimony relates to two people, by making them one, it follows that for the one sacrament of marriage to be received by both parties, it is necessary that both of them have been baptized. When both parties are baptized, all other things being equal, this couple can confer on each other the sacrament of matrimony. We must now consider the situation when one of the parties to the marriage is not baptized.

That the Pope sets aside non-sacramental unions—for good reasons—can be established from the history of the Church. There have been countless examples of the Popes exercising this power. It is important, however, that this power of the Pope to set aside the union of a couple wherein one of the parties has not been baptized is carefully distinguished from the Pauline Privilege. The Pauline Privilege is based on the text of the first letter of St. Paul to the Corinthians (Chapter 7, vs. 8–15). Here, the Apostle is thought to be speaking of the situation in which two pagans marry, and subsequently one of them receives the sacrament of baptism. Thereafter, the unbaptised party refuses to live peacefully with the Christian party, without 'offence to the Creator', and does not wish himself to be baptized. In such circumstances, provided these last three conditions can be properly established (i.e. baptism of one party, refusal to live peacefully, and no conversion of the other party) the Christian party is permitted by the bishop of the place to proceed to a new marriage. It is held that the first marriage is dissolved by the 'exercise of the Pauline Privilege'.

In the procedure relating to the Pauline Privilege, it must be clearly established that the couple cannot live together. To ascertain this, the non-Christian party may be questioned, or perhaps there may already be a divorce, which would demonstrate the couple's irreconcilability. Although this type of case is relatively simple, it does not happen very frequently in Western Europe. On the other hand, in countries where Christian baptism is rare, the exercise of the Pauline Privilege is more frequent. However, regardless of the frequency of the use of the Pauline Privilege, it will be noticed that this procedure differs considerably from the 'dissolution of the natural bond' with which we now deal.

In the dissolution of the natural bond—which is sometimes called the *Petrine Privilege*, or the extension of the Pauline Privilege, or the dissolution *in favour of the faith*—it must be established that *one* of the parties to the original marriage was not baptized. When this can be shown with certainty, it follows that the marriage in question was not a sacrament. Where this is the case, in certain circumstances a petition may be put to the Holy Father asking that the former union be dissolved in *favour of the faith* of the Catholic party who is now involved.

The Holy See at present will accept a petition from an unbaptised person who now wishes to marry a Catholic; from a previously unbaptised person, now baptised as a non-Catholic, and who wishes to marry a Catholic; from a previously unbaptised person, now a Catholic, who wishes to marry another Catholic, or at least a baptised non-Catholic; and also from a Catholic previously married to an unbaptised person (with a dispensation from disparity of cult) who now wishes to marry another baptised person. However currently the Holy See will not accept a request from a baptised petitioner, previously married to an unbaptised person, and who having been received into the Church, wishes to marry another unbaptised person.

When a person petitions the Holy Father for a dissolution of a marriage on the grounds that one of the parties to the union was not baptised, there are two basic requirements. Firstly, it must be established that the person concerned was not baptized at the time of the marriage and, if he was subsequently baptized, that the couple did not live together as man and wife after the baptism. Secondly, there must be adequate reasons why the Holy Father is asked to dissolve the union.

## PROOF OF NON-BAPTISM

It is, of course, extremely difficult to prove that something did not happen—indeed it is a logical impossibility. This, to some extent, explains the reason why a natural bond case takes as long as it does. However, in spite of the difficulties, it is possible to become morally certain that a baptism did not take place. The whole process concerning the natural bond of marriage is governed by a special

Instruction of the Sacred Congregation for the Doctrine of the Faith (the new name for the Holy Office). There are two basic features to this proof. The positive feature is that 'evidence' must be taken from persons who would have been in a position to know whether the child was baptised. For example, the child's parents, or close relatives such as aunts and uncles. It is necessary that whoever does give evidence should have known the person concerned in childhood. For example, it is hardly worthwhile obtaining the evidence of an uncle who lived abroad throughout the person's childhood. He would not be in a position to state anything useful about the non-baptism. Basically, therefore, it means that the witnesses must be the parents or failing them the very close relatives with whom the child was brought up.

Evidence is taken from these persons under oath, and the questioning seeks to establish not merely that the witness knows that the child was not baptized, but that he can also state why not. The reason for a child not being baptised can add considerably to the likelihood, or the reverse, of the facts alleged. The questions would establish the relationship of the witness to the one alleged to be unbaptised: how close the witness was to the child; why he would have known about a baptism if one had taken place; whether the child had been in hospital, or had any serious illness; had taken part in any church activities—Sunday School, cubs, choir, etc; had worshipped in any churches; and such questions as to establish the possibility, the reasons, the likelihood of the alleged non-baptism. The petitioner is also questioned. All the witnesses and the petitioner are questioned concerning the marriage which is alleged to be non-sacramental. It is necessary to establish how it broke down—for example, whether the petitioner was the malicious cause of the breakdown. If he was, it would be very unlikely indeed that a dissolution would be granted.

Following upon this positive evidence, a certain amount of negative evidence must be obtained. Negative evidence is obtained by conducting searches in the baptismal records of the churches in the areas where the person lived from the time of birth to the time of the marriage and even afterwards, if necessary. That is in the places where it is likely (or reasonable to believe) that the person could have been baptised. It will be appreciated that baptismal searches can never establish that a person was not baptised. They will merely establish that there is no record of a baptism in the registers of the churches searched. Moreover, this leaves open the possibility that the minister of the baptism did not enter the record of the baptism into the register. Since it is not possible to search every baptismal register everywhere, it follows that searching merely constitutes corroborative evidence of the positive testimony which has been obtained from the witnesses.

It may be thought that this type of corroborative evidence is not important. On the contrary, almost every tribunal has had the experience when the parents of a child have stated under oath that their child was never baptised, and after careful searches, evidence of baptism is discovered. Sometimes the parents may have just forgotten; on other occasions it can become clear that the witnesses were deliberately lying so as to mislead the tribunal. Obviously great care must be taken with cases such as this, so that if a dissolution is finally granted, it is clear beyond all reasonable doubt, the person concerned was never baptised.

## THE ACTUAL PROCEDURE

When someone approaches a tribunal, and wishes to submit a petition on the grounds that his or her marriage was not a sacrament, the first step taken by the tribunal is to assist the person concerned to formulate a petition. This sets down the brief facts concerning the marriage, why it took place, why it broke down; and details concerning the alleged non-baptism. The names and addresses of witnesses, of the kind mentioned above, are also obtained. The petitioner is subsequently asked to give sworn evidence. In addition to the questions about the marriage and about the alleged non-baptism, he is also asked if he is quite clear that if the Apostolic Dissolution is obtained as a result of perjury any subsequent union would be null and void. The evidence is taken under oath.

Thereafter, the witnesses named, wherever they may be, are also questioned. At the same time, baptismal searches are carried out. When the evidence of the witnesses and the relevant documents have been obtained[1], and the results of the baptismal searches collated, all the material is transcribed. It is then submitted to the 'defender of the bond'. The latter examines the dossier, and sees whether all possible steps have been taken to establish the non-baptism. If he considers that more should be done to cover certain possibilities, he has the right to ask for these further enquiries to be made. It can happen that as a result of these further investigations, the baptism of the person concerned is discovered. When the 'defender of the bond' is satisfied that everything necessary has

---

[1]    Amongst these documents will be a civil divorce or nullity decree absolute. It is very unusual for a case to be started until the petitioner has been divorced. This prevents complications in civil law. The point applies equally to nullity and non-consummation cases.

been done, he returns the dossier to the tribunal with his comments on the case.

Then the dossier, with the comments of the 'defender of the bond', is submitted to the bishop of the diocese. He writes his 'opinion' on the case showing whether he is convinced by the evidence supplied, and stating whether in view of the merits (or otherwise) of the petitioner, he recommends the case to the Holy Father. The case and bishop's opinion are then sent to the Sacred Congregation for the Doctrine of the Faith, where three specially appointed commissioners and one 'defender of the bond' examine the case. If the authorities are satisfied that the alleged non-baptism has been established, and that the merits of the petitioner warrant it, the case is then recommended to the Holy Father. The Pope personally grants the dissolution of the natural bond of marriage. There may be certain conditions attached to the dissolution. Occasionally the Congregation may ask for more information, and this must be supplied before the case can go further.

This, then, is a brief outline of the procedure that is required for the conduct of the natural bond case. We must now deal with certain points that arise.

THE KIND OF BAPTISM

In speaking about baptism we are of course concerned with Christian baptism—that is, with a valid baptism. Thus, for example, to say the words, 'I baptize you in the name of the Father, of the Son and of the Holy Ghost' whilst not using water is regarded as an invalid baptism. Then again there are certain baptisms, so called, which are either non-trinitarian, or else make no pretence at the ceremony of Christian initiation as normally understood. Again, such would not constitute baptism in the sense in which we are here discussing it.

But having said this, it will be realised at once that it is exceedingly difficult to establish that something described as a 'baptism' or 'Christening' was not a valid form of the ceremony. Usually natural bond cases arise many years after the birth of the person, and hence it is not very likely that there would be evidence to demonstrate the invalidity of the baptism to the full satisfaction of the Congregation. Nonetheless, it is a factor to keep in mind: that non-baptism, in fact, refers to the absence of Christian baptism, to give it its proper title.

DISSOLUTION IS A FAVOUR, NOT A RIGHT

It will be understood that what we have been saying is that a petition for dissolution refers to what is normally regarded as a valid marriage. For this reason, whether or not the Holy Father chooses to dissolve a certain marriage is a matter for his decision alone. The mere fact it is established that a person has not been baptized does not constitute a right to the dissolution of the union in question. There are a variety of factors that are involved.

The first of these factors is whether the merits of the petitioner warrant the favour of the dissolution. We have already mentioned that a case will not be entertained if the petitioner has been the malicious cause of the breakdown of the marriage. We can give an example of this. Henry, an unbaptised person, is married. The marriage is not as happy as it might be, nonetheless it does exist as a bond between two people. Then he meets a Catholic girl. Through his friendship with this girl, his own married relationship begins to deteriorate even further, and as a result he turns more and more to the Catholic girl for comfort in the situation in which he finds himself. Then he commits adultery with the girl. Not long afterwards, his wife discovers this and after some period of argument and dispute, the wife separates from, and divorces her husband. Henry becomes a Catholic, and then tries to present a petition for the dissolution of his marriage. In such a case, it is clear that Henry, through neglect of his own marriage, has allowed the relationship between him and his wife to be severed, and the Catholic girl is probably equally culpable. It is more than likely that he would not be allowed to petition for a dissolution for the purpose of marrying the Catholic girl. If the Holy Father were to dissolve the marriage so as to allow the two to marry, it would certainly seem as if the Church was condoning the dereliction of marital duties and obligations. This could not be allowed. Hence, it is necessary to establish as part of this type of case, that the petitioner and the person he wishes to marry were not responsible for the breakdown of the marriage. Stringent questioning on this issue may be necessary, but the ultimate aim is to establish the true situation concerning the breakdown of the marriage. Moreover, it must also be clear that even when the petitioner was not the cause of the breakdown of the marriage, that subsequent to the breakdown he is fulfilling his natural obligations by maintaining his wife and any children.

The next factor to be considered before the Holy Father can entertain the possibility of granting a dissolution is the reason for asking the favour. The basic reason for this is that the granting of the dissolution would be in favour of the faith of the Catholic party involved in the case. This is something which will be carefully evaluated both by the local tribunal and by the Congregation in Rome.

The third consideration to be taken into account before the petition can be granted is the question of scandal. Obviously we have to draw a distinction here between two sorts of scandal. There is one kind which really does create a situation which might lead a person into sin—for example, when a child sees an older person doing something, it could well lead to the child considering this action to be in order, at least after an initial period of surprise. In this sense, scandal is the possible cause of someone sinning. On the other hand, scandal is also the term used to describe a certain surprise arising in a person due to a lack of instruction or understanding of Catholicism. For instance,.the term scandal could be used relating to the situation when someone learns that a neighbour has been granted a decree of nullity. The scandal arises from the fact that the one scandalised did not realise that there has existed grounds for nullity. Obviously the term scandal is being used here in quite another sense.

In connection with the Holy Father granting a dissolution of the natural bond of a marriage, there might exist certain circumstances which could lead to scandal in the proper sense of the word. For example, it might be well known that the petitioner was the malicious cause of the breakdown of his marriage. Scandal might well be caused if, as a result of the dissolution, he married the girl with whom he had committed adultery during his first marriage. In such a case, the Holy Father would not grant a dissolution. On the other hand, the petitioner may have led a most exemplary life, and it was his first wife who really acted unjustly in the marriage. She finally ran off with another man leaving the husband with three small children. If the conditions for a natural bond of marriage were established, then the Holy Father might grant the dissolution, in spite of the fact that someone who was not aware of the teaching of the Church about the dissolution of non-sacramental unions might raise his eyebrows at the granting of the dissolution.

It will be seen, therefore, that before a petition can be sent to Rome, there must have been most careful enquiries made concerning the possibility of scandal; and questions are asked of numerous persons about this. The bishop must be well aware of the facts; and he must cause enquiries to be made into the matter to discover the precise situation concerning the possibility of scandal. The obvious purpose of such enquiries is to prevent harm to souls.

We have now seen the basic outline of the natural bond case. This is a case which will vary in frequency depending upon the country or the area. Naturally, in places where there is a very large Catholic population, the bishop will be much more loth to recommend a case to the Holy Father than in a place where there are fewer Catholics.

The bishop is the sole judge of the circumstances concerning the possibility of scandal arising from the granting of the dissolution. He is the one, who recommends (or not) a case to Rome. Furthermore, the frequency of this type of case depends largely on whether there are a large number of people in the country who are not baptised. The basic principle of the natural bond case, like that of the non-consummation case, is that it is a favour not a right. Hence it is within the competence and authority of the Holy Father alone to decide whether or not to grant a case in the specific circumstances. It will be readily understood that the circumstances in every case are different, but that only a few people will be knowledgeable as to what the precise facts are. Frequently people assume that their case is 'like so and so's case'. If all the facts of both cases were available it is highly likely that the two cases are not at all similar. The position is made more difficult by the fact that the personal details of the marriages of the different parties are closely guarded secrets, and must remain such. For this reason, it is always as well to consult the local tribunal rather than to formulate private opinions on the facts.

It has been the purpose of this little book to try to describe the more intricate details involved in the handling of marriage cases by the tribunals of the Church. It has not been the aim to attempt a legal treatise on the various aspects of the law, but merely to provide a short and practical manual to be of assistance to those trying to understand the workings of the Church's marriage tribunals. More detailed information can only come from personal consultation with tribunals and canon lawyers.

# APPENDIX:

## DOCUMENTS OF THE HOLY SEE

Various references have been made in this little book to documents
of the Holy See which govern various aspects of the procedure we
have described. In due time much of the material in most of these
documents will be absorbed into the appropriate sections of the new
*Code of Canon Law*. However since it is unlikely that the new Code
will be promulgated for some time to come, it may be useful for
students and others to have some of these more relevant documents
set out. At the moment the documents themselves are published in
the official Bulletin in the Church, the *Acta Apostolicae Sedis* in
latin, and therefore are not immediately accessible.

The documents set out in this appendix are first of all the *motu
proprio* of Pope Paul VI issued on 27 March 1971 and called *Causas
Matrimoniales*. The background to this document was this. For
some years applications had been made to the Holy See from
various countries for modifications in the procedure of nullity
cases and those which dealt with the natural bond and non-
consummation. In certain cases special permissions concerning
various points were issued by the Holy See; but they differed for
different countries, depending principally upon what has been
requested as well as on the special circumstances obtaining in each
country. Thus special variations were granted to England and
Wales; others to Canada, the United States, Australia, Belgium, to
name but a few. As a result of this the Holy See decided to
standardize where necessary these various aspects of the procedure.
In March 1971 a special document, a *motu proprio* i.e. from the Pope
himself, was issued which was designed to standardize various
elements of the procedure of nullity cases; this was the document
*Causas Matrimoniales*. This had effect throughout the whole world;
although the Holy See still allowed variations from this procedure
in the United States and in Canada where it was considered that
special circumstances prevailed, due to size, the number of
Catholics, and the paucity of trained Canon Lawyers. The *motu
proprio* is set out here; and also following it are the special
regulations that were permitted to remain in force in the United
States.

These special norms for the United States were originally

granted on 28 April 1970, for three years; they were renewed for a further year on 20 June 1973; and then in 1974 the Holy See permitted (subject to a few modifications) these same norms to remain in force until such time as the section of the new Code on procedure in such cases is promulgated. Still at this time, however, the precise operation of two of the special norms is under discussion between the United States Hierarchy and the Holy See.

Not only were special faculties and permissions being requested by various countries in connection with nullity procedures, but also in non-consummation cases as well. Consequently the Holy See also standardized the procedure here, and issued a document to this effect on 7 March 1972. The substance of this document is also reproduced.

In the case of natural bond petitions, there is a slightly different background. Towards the end of the nineteen sixties, the Congregation for the Doctrine of the Faith instituted a special examination of the procedures being used; but even more, a detailed examination of the nature of the petition that would be accepted by the Holy See. Prior to this, the Congregation had accepted cases, for example, from a Catholic party who had previously been married to an unbaptised person with a dispensation from disparity of cult, and who now wanted to marry (following a dissolution) *another* unbaptised person. It will be seen that what would be happening here is for the Catholic party to be allowed to enter into a *series* of dissoluble unions! Consequently the Congregation for the Doctrine of the Faith set up a special commission of theologians to examine the matter to see whether the Holy Father even had the power to grant such favours. In the meanwhile all such cases were suspended. Then on 6 December 1973 the Congregation—having received a report from the special commission of theologians—issued an Instruction on the procedure now required for natural bond cases, also setting out precisely from whom petitions would be accepted. This document is also set out in this appendix.


**DOCUMENT I:**     The instructions of the *motu proprio* 'Causas Matrimoniales': 27 March 1971 (Ref: AAS 1971, Vol. 63, p.441)

### THE COMPETENT FORUM
I.        The marriage cases of the baptized by proper right pertain to an ecclesiastical judge.

II.        Cases concerning the merely civil effects of marriage are the concern of the civil authorities, unless particular law lays down that such cases, if they are dealt with in an incidental and accessory manner, may be examined and decided by an ecclesiastical judge.

III.      All marriage cases concerning those persons mentioned in the *Code of Canon Law*, can. 1557, §1, n.1, are judged by the Congregation, Tribunal, or special Commission to which the Supreme Pontiff entrusts them in each case.

IV.       §1. In other cases concerning the nullity of marriage the competent body is:

      a)   the tribunal of the place in which the marriage was celebrated; or

      b)   the tribunal of the place in which the respondent has an abode which is not transitory, which may be proved from some ecclesiastical document or in some other legitimate manner; or

      c)   the tribunal of the place in which *de facto* most of the depositions or proofs have to be collected, provided the consent is obtained both of the Ordinary of the place where the respondent habitually lives and of the Ordinary of the place in which the tribunal approached is situated, and of the president of the tribunal itself.

      §2.   If the circumstances mentioned in §1.c) above occur, the tribunal, before admitting the case must inquire of the respondent whether he or she has any objection to the forum approached by the petitioner.

      §3.   Should there occur a substantial change in the circumstances, places or persons mentioned in §1, the cause, before its closure, may be transferred in particular cases from one tribunal to another equally competent one, provided both parties and both tribunals agree.

## THE CONSTITUTION OF TRIBUNALS

V.        §1.    If it is impossible either in a diocesan tribunal or, where one is set up, in a regional tribunal, to form a college of three clerical judges, the episcopal conference is given the faculty of permitting in the first and second instance the appointment of a college composed of two clerics and one layman.

§2.   In the first instance, when a college as described in §1 cannot be set up even by adding a layman, in individual instances, cases concerning the nullity of marriage may be entrusted by the episcopal conference to one cleric as the sole judge. Such a judge where possible will choose an assessor and auditor for the case.

§3.   The episcopal conference can, in accordance with its statutes, grant the above-mentioned faculties either through a group of members or at least one member of the conference, to be chosen for this purpose.

VI.   For the office of assessor and auditor in tribunals of any instance laymen may be used. The office of notary may be accepted by both men and woman.

VII.   Lay people chosen for these offices should be outstanding in their Catholic faith and good character as well as their knowledge of canon law. When it is a question of conferring the office of judge upon a layman, as laid down in V, §1, those who have legal experience are to be preferred.

## APPEALS

VIII.   §1.   The 'defender of the bond' is obliged to appeal to the higher tribunal, within the time laid down by law, against a first sentence declaring the nullity of a marriage. If he fails to do this, he shall be compelled to do so by the authority of the president or the sole judge.

§2.   Before the tribunal of second instance, the 'defender of the bond' shall produce his observations stating whether or not he has any objection to make against the decision made in the first instance. The college shall, if it thinks it opportune, ask for the observations of the parties or of their advocates against those made by the 'defender of the bond'.

§3.   Having examined the sentence and having considered the observations of the 'defender of the bond' and, if they were asked for and given, those of the parties or of their advocates, the college by its decree shall either ratify the decision of the first instance, or admit the case to the ordinary examination of the second instance. In the first of the two cases, if no one makes recourse, the couple, provided there is no other impediment, have the right to contract a new marriage after ten days have elapsed from the publication of the decree.

IX.      §1.   If the decree of the college ratifies the first-instance sentence, the 'defender of the bond' or a party who believes himself to be aggrieved has the right to make recourse to a higher tribunal within ten days from the date of publication of the decree, provided he presents new and serious arguments. These arguments must be placed before the third-instance tribunal within a month from making recourse.

§2.   The 'defender of the bond' of the third instance, after hearing the president of the tribunal, can withdraw from the recourse, and in that case the tribunal shall declare the case terminated. If it is a party who makes recourse, the tribunal having considered the arguments adduced, within a month from the making of recourse shall either reject it by decree or admit the case to ordinary examination in the third instance.

## RULES IN SPECIAL CASES

X.      When there is proof from a certain and authentic document, not subject to any contradiction or exception, that a diriment impediment exists, and when it is also equally certain and clear that no dispensation from this impediment has been given, in these cases the formalities laid down in law can be omitted and the Ordinary, after the parties have been summoned and the 'defender of the bond' has intervened, can declare the marriage null.

XI.      With the same provisions and in the same manner as in n. X, the Ordinary can declare a marriage null also when the case was entered into on the grounds of lack of canonical form or lack of a valid mandate on the part of the proxy.

XII.      If the 'defender of the bond' prudently considers that the impediments or defects mentioned in nn.X and XI are not certain or that it is probable that there was a dispensation from them, he is bound to appeal against this declaration to the judge of second instance. The proceedings are to be transmitted to him and he is to be notified in writing that the case is a special one.

XIII.      The judge of second instance, with the sole intervention of the 'defender of the bond', shall decide in the same way as in n.X whether the sentence is to be confirmed or whether the case is to be proceeded with through the ordinary channels of law. In this latter case he shall send it back to the tribunal of first instance.

## TRANSITIONAL NORMS

1. On the day on which the present apostolic letter comes into force, a marriage case which is proceeding before a higher tribunal by reason of lawful appeal after a first sentence declaring the marriage null shall be temporarily suspended.[1]

2. The 'defender of the bond' of the tribunal of second instance shall make his observations on all that concerns either the decision given in the first instance or the proceedings completed in the second instance up to that date, and thereby state whether or not he has any objection to make against the decision made in the first instance. The college shall, if it thinks it opportune, ask for the observations of the parties or of their advocates against these observations.

3. Having considered the observations of the 'defender of the bond' and, if they were asked for and given, those of the parties or of their advocates, and having examined the sentence of the first instance, the college by its decree shall either ratify the first-instance decision or decide that the case must be proceeded with by examination in the second instance. In the former case, if no one makes recourse, the couple have the right, provided there is no other impediment, to contract a new marriage after ten days have elapsed from the publication of the decree. In the latter case the instance must be proceeded with until the definitive sentence is given.

We order that all that is decreed in this letter issued by us *motu proprio* be valid and firm, anything to the contrary notwithstanding, even if worthy of most special mention.

**DOCUMENT II:**    The procedural norms for the USA granted 28 April 1970; renewed and in force until the promulgation of *De Processibus* of the new *Code of Canon Law*.

1.  The diocesan tribunal will consist of judges, a 'defender of the bond', a 'promotor of justice' and notaries and all will be appointed to their offices by the Ordinary. The judges, defenders of the bond and promotor of justice shall be priests; all, however, shall be endowed with those qualities required by law.

---

[1]   The *motu proprio* came into effect on 1st October 1971.

2. The Ordinary will appoint a chief judge who will direct the work of the tribunal and assign judges and defenders of the bond for individual cases.

3. A collegiate tribunal must be constituted for each case. The Episcopal Conference, in accordance with faculties to be sought from the Holy See, may permit the competent ecclesiastical tribunal to derogate from this norm for a specified period of time, so that a case may be handled by a single judge.

   The conditions are that: 1) there be a grave reason for granting the derogation; and 2) no formal opposition be expressed prior to the definitive sentence by either the judge, the 'defender of the bond', the 'promotor of justice' or either of the parties.

4. If both parties are desirous of a declaration of nullity, one advocate may represent both. Unless a party decides otherwise, the advocate in first instance will also be the advocate in second instance. Advocates representing the parties will be those approved to work with marriage cases by the Ordinary or his delegate.

5. The notary for the tribunal will preserve a written record of all procedural and substantive acts, with special regard to names, dates and places as well as the authenticity of documents and depositions. While acts not authenticated by the notary are null, it suffices that copies of these acts be authenticated by a single statement of the notary at the termination of the case.

6. The Ordinary will provide sufficient judges, defenders and advocates so that all petitions for declarations of nullity may be accepted or rejected promptly and decisions given within six months following acceptance of the petition.

7. The first competent tribunal to which a party presents a petition has an obligation to accept or reject the petition. The competence of a tribunal of first instance shall be determined by the residence of either party to the marriage, the place of the marriage or the decree of the judge to whom the petition is presented that his tribunal is better able to judge the case than any other tribunal. In this last instance, however, the judge may not issue such a decree without first obtaining the consent of his own Ordinary and the consent of the petitioner's Ordinary and chief judge.

8. Any spouse, without qualification, may seek a declaration of nullity of his marriage. To do so, he will employ the services of an advocate. The petition for the declaration of nullity indicating the basis or bases for nullity and the sources of proof is to be accepted or rejected by the judge within the thirty days following the presentation and after consultation with the advocate and defender. Recourse against the rejection of a petition may be made to the tribunal of second instance. Within thirty days of recourse, rejection of the petition is to be sustained or the case is to be remanded for prompt instruction by the tribunal of first instance.

9. The 'promotor of justice' may petition that a marriage be declared null when he decides this will be for the public good.

10. If he is available and cooperative, the respondent will be given the opportunity of choosing an advocate prior to the determination of the precise basis for nullity. If the respondent is not available and cooperative, the judge will proceed to this determination in accordance with the following rule.

11. Within a month of the acceptance of the petition, the judge, after consultation with the advocate and defender, will determine the precise basis or bases for the nullity of the marriage, the documents to be obtained, and the witnesses to be heard. During the course of the trial the judge may add additional grounds of nullity.

12. At any time in the course of the trial, the petitioner may request that the case be transferred from one competent tribunal to another competent tribunal. This permission will be granted provided that a grave reason warrants it, that the 'defender of the bond' has been heard and that it is agreeable to the other party, to the Ordinary *a quo* and to the chief judges of both tribunals.

13. The testimony of the principal and the witnesses will be taken by the judges as soon as available, either at the tribunal or elsewhere. A person will be asked to take an oath before testifying unless the judge determines otherwise. The advocate (unless the judge determines otherwise) and the defender have the right to be present at the hearing of the

principals and witnesses. In the event that the advocate is present, the 'defender of the bond' must always at least be cited. The questions proposed by the judge will be based upon the information and questions supplied by the advocate and the defender. The principals and witnesses may also be questioned directly by the advocate and the defender under the direction of the judge. When a judge is personally unable to take the testimony of a witness, he will appoint a competent delegate to do so.

14. Following consultation with the advocate and defender, the judge will determine the significance of the unwillingness of a principal and/or witness to testify and will, if necessary, proceed to the conclusion of the case without their testimony.

15. The advocate and the defender may examine the acts of the case at any stage of the process unless in particular cases the judge decides otherwise.

16. The judge will carefully weigh the depositions of each witness. Testimonials concerning the credibility of the principals and witnesses will be required if, in the opinion of the judge, they seem necessary or useful.

17. In cases involving physical or psychic impotence and lack of consentual capacity, the judge, after consultation with the advocate and the defender shall designate one or more experts to study the acts of the case and submit a written report thereon. When advisable, this expert will examine the party or parties to the case and will include in his report the results of his examination. The oral testimony of the expert is to be taken only if his report requires clarification or implementation. Following consultation with the advocate and the defender, the judge may appoint additional experts.

18. When, after consultation with the advocate and the defender, the judge has decided that all necessary and available evidence has been obtained, the principals will be permitted to read the acts, unless, in the opinion of the judge, there is danger of violation of the rights of privacy. The judge will consider the requests by the principals for further instruction before bringing the case to a conclusion.

19. The advocate and the defender will submit written comments

independently within one month after all the evidence has been presented and will be given the opportunity of a reply to be made within two weeks.

20. Following whatever consultation with the advocate and the defender which is allowed by law and which he deems necessary, the judge will render a decision within one month after the presentation of the written comments and replies.

21. The judge will render his decision according to moral certitude generated by the prevailing weight of that evidence having a recognised value in law and jurisprudence.

22. Any instance of nullity as defined in positive law with regard to acts or processes is considered sanated by the sentence itself provided that it was not previously challenged.

    A sentence is irremediably null only when: 1) Its pre-suppositions were lacking grounds; 2) the right of defence has been denied; 3) the judge was coerced either by violence or grave fear to render his decision; 4) the sentence fails to address itself to the controversy in question.

    The nullity described in the paragraph above may be perpetually proposed either as an action or as an exception.

23. I.   Once an appeal has been made to a higher tribunal and the tribunal itself has been constituted in accord with Norm 3, the citation of the parties and the joining of issues shall take place within one month.

    At the time of the joining of issues, if further investigations are requested either by the parties or the 'defender of the bond' or the tribunal itself *ex officio,* the case shall be heard in the ordinary manner of second instance. This instance, however, should not if possible exceed the limit of six months.

    If further investigations are not required, the judge will immediately decree the case concluded. Within a month from the date of this decree, the tribunal, taking into account the pleadings and animadversions of the advocate and 'defender of the bond', shall issue a new sentence according to the norm of the law.

    II. In those exceptional cases where in the judgement of the 'defender of the bond' and his Ordinary an appeal against an affirmative decision would clearly be superfluous, the Ordinary may himself request of the Episcopal Conference that in these individual cases the 'defender of the bond' be dispensed from the obligation to appeal so that the sentence of the first instance may be executed immediately.

**DOCUMENT III:**    Special instructions of the Congregation of the Sacraments dealing with alterations in the procedure for Non-consummation cases, dated 7 March 1972. (Ref: AAS Vol. 64, p.244 ff.)

## I  GENERAL FACULTY TO CONDUCT THE PROCESS SUPER RATO ET NON CONSUMMATO

It pertains exclusively to the Congregation of the Sacraments to examine the fact of non-consummation of marriage not only between Catholic parties, whether of the Latin or Eastern Churches, but also between a Catholic party and a non-Catholic party and between baptized non-Catholics, as well as to examine the existence of a just or proportionately serious cause for the granting of the pontifical favor of a dissolution.

By force of this instruction all diocesan bishops have the general faculty, for their own territory, to conduct the *super matrimonio rato et non consummato* process from the day when this instruction comes into effect until the promulgation of the revised *Code of Canon Law*, so that they no longer need to seek this faculty from the Apostolic See. In using this faculty the bishops should take into account articles 7 and 8 of the *Regulae Servandae* and carefully observe the following prescriptions:

a)  The process is not judicial but administrative, and therefore it differs from the judicial process for cases of nullity. In the process a simple petition is made for a favor to be obtained from the concession of the Supreme Pontiff. Nevertheless, in view of the gravity of the matter, the truth of the fact of non-consummation is to be sought no less religiously and diligently than in strictly judicial matters, so that the Pope may use his supreme power with full knowledge of the case. It is for the properly deputed Instructing Judge, therefore, to gather proofs of non-consummation and of the existence of a just or proportionately serious cause for the concession of the favor. If from an examination of the acts of the process insufficient proofs are found, the Congregation may suggest to the bishop, according to circumstances, that the proofs be completed in accord with appropriate instructions.

b)  Only the spouses may seek the dissolution; both may seek it or either one, even against the will of the other. Although it is the right of any member of the faithful to send the petition (which is always to be addressed to the Supreme Pontiff) directly to the Apostolic See it is expedient and always recommended that it be presented to the bishop. After considering the matter, he will see to the conduct of the process. Whenever it is a petition of one party alone, the other is to be heard extra-judicially before the process is begun, unless in particular cases another course seems opportune.

c) Before the process is conducted the bishop must be certain of the juridical basis of the petition and the opportuneness of undertaking the process. Likewise he should not fail to encourage the reconciliation of the parties, if this is possible, through the removal of the reasons for aversion and dissension, unless the facts and personal circumstances indicate that such an attempt would be useless.

d) The bishop should refer to the Congregation complicated cases or those with special difficulties of the juridical or moral order. The Congregation will weigh carefully all the circumstances and will communicate to the bishop the steps to be taken.

e) If it happens that a prudent doubt arises, from the examination of the petition, concerning the validity of the marriage, then it is for the bishop either to counsel the petitioner to follow the judicial order (or a declaration of nullity, in accord with the law) or—provided the petition is based on a solid and juridical foundation—to permit the *super rato et non consummato* process to be conducted. When, however, a case of nullity has been prosecuted on the grounds of impotence and, in the judgement of the tribunal, proof not of impotence but of non-consummation has emerged from the acts and evidence, then, upon the petition of one or both parties for an apostolic dissolution, all the acts should be sent to the Congregation together with the animadversions of the 'defender of the bond' and the *votum* of the tribunal and the bishop, based on legal and especially factual arguments. With regard to the *votum*, the bishop may follow that of the tribunal and add his signature to it, with the assurance of a just or proportionately serious cause for the dissolution, and the absence of scandal. If in the judgement of the tribunal, insufficient proofs of non-consummation have been obtained up to this point, in accord with the *Regulae Servandae* of May 7 1923, the proofs should be completed by the instructing judge and the completed acts sent to the Congregation with the animadversions of the 'defender of the bond' and the *votum* of the tribunal and the bishop. If it is a question of another ground of nullity (e.g. defect of consent, force and fear, etc) and in the judgement of the tribunal the nullity cannot be established but incidentally a very probable doubt emerges about non-consummation, it is the right of one or both parties to present a petition for dissolution to the Supreme Pontiff and the instructing judge has the right to conduct the case in accord with the norms in the *Regulae Servandae*. Then all the acts, as above, should be sent to the Congregation together with the usual animadversions of the 'defender of the bond' and the *votum* of the tribunal and the bishop.

f) The bishop must be vigilant lest the parties, witnesses, or experts give false depositions or withhold the truth. He knows—and through him all interested persons should know—that the favor of dissolution cannot be granted unless two things are proved: that the marriage was actually not consummated and that a just or proportionately serious cause exists; in the absence of either or both the rescript is affected by *obreptio* and can in no way work to the advantage of the one who obtains it. It is clear that the pontifical dissolution never becomes definitive and a new marriage which may be entered after an invalid dissolution can always be declared null, if it later becomes known that the first marriage was actually *ratum et consummatum*.

## II   CONDUCT OF THE CASE AND THE ACTS

With regard to the conduct of the case, the inquiry to establish accurately and expeditiously, whether it is true that the marriage was not consummated should foster the holiness and indissolubility of marriage. It therefore seems that the following emendations should be introduced in the norms for these processes in the *Code of Canon Law* and the *Regulae Servandae* of the Congregation for the Discipline of the Sacraments:

a) If, because of the size of the diocese or eparchy and especially because of the lack of priests who are expert in canon law, it is difficult to conduct the *super rato* process in the *curia* or tribunal, the bishop may, after prudent consideration and especially in more difficult cases, transfer his competence to conduct the process to the ministers of the regional, provincial, interdiocesan, or interritual tribunal (if any) or of the tribunal of a nearby diocese or eparchy which is capable of undertaking the process.

b) In cases of non-consummation both spouses must present witnesses who can testify to their probity and especially to their truthfulness with reference to the asserted non-consummation; the instructing judge may add other witnesses *ex officio*. A few witnesses may suffice, provided their concordant testimony can give valid proof and moral certitude. This is the case if they are persons above suspicion, agree among themselves, and testify under oath: indicating when, how, and what they heard from the spouses or their close relatives about the non-consummation. It should not be forgotten that in these cases the moral argument is of great weight in attaining moral certitude concerning non-consummation.

c) The physical examination is to be employed if necessary for juridical proof of the fact of non-consummation. If, however, in accord with the decree of the Congregation of the Holy Office of June 12 1942, the bishop judges there is full proof in view of the moral excellence of the parties and witnesses, after serious consideration of their spiritual disposition and other supporting arguments, the medical examination may be omitted; all these matters should be weighed before the examination is decreed to be useless. If the woman refuses the physical examination, in accord with the rule of the above decree the examination should not be insisted upon. Finally, with regard to this examination, patriarchal synods and episcopal conferences have the faculty to establish additional norms according to local and other circumstances.

d) The procedural acts must be in writing and must be certified by notaries. With the bishop's consent the *curia* or tribunal may use tape recorders, in accord with current practice and technical progress, if their use seems to be useful and suitable for making a more accurate and certain record of the acts. The acts, however, may be given credence only if, although taken down by tape recorder, they satisfy the prescriptions expressly required by the law.

e) Differently from cases of nullity, because of the special nature of the *super rato* process, the assistance of advocates and procurators may not be sought. In response to the recommendations and desires of some pastors, however, it is decreed that the parties—at their own request or by *ex officio* decree of the bishop—may use the services of counsellors or experts, especially ecclesiastics, in these cases. These may assist in drawing up petitions, in the conduct of the case, or in completing the acts of the process. Thus the good of souls may be assured more certainly, while the truth of non-consummation is protected. The designation of counsellors or experts, whether chosen *ex officio* or at the request of the parties, pertains to the bishop after he has heard the 'defender of the bond' and informed the counsellors or experts beforehand. This is done by a special decree and with the requirement of secrecy lest the procedural acts become known to outsiders.

f) In writing the *votum pro rei veritate,* bishops should weigh the nature and qualities of the case in a concrete and practical manner, that is, by considering the special circumstances of the persons, the fact of non-consummation, and the opportuneness of the concession.

In cases of nullity, when the acts are sent to the Congregation for a dissolution (cf. n.I, e), or of non-consummation which are conducted with an extension of competence (cf. n.II, a), the archbishop or metropolitan of the regional, provincial, inter-diocesan, interritual, tribunal or the bishop of the neighbouring diocese or eparchy should before writing his *votum,* consult with the bishop of the petitioner who knows the conditions of his diocese or eparchy, at least with regard to the scandal which may arise from a pontifical dissolution. If the bishop judges that the scandal arises or has arisen without basis or reason, then he should try to prevent it or contain it with pastoral care and appropriate means.

g) All the procedural acts, both of the case and of the process, together with other documents which are not in Latin, may be drawn up in those venacular languages that are widely used. Judicial acts and documents drawn up in a language that is not well known may be translated into one of the above languages.

The procedural acts and documents are to be sent to the Congregation in three copies, which may be photostatic copies, with certification of authenticity, the original manuscript shall be preserved in the archives of the *curia* or tribunal and is to be submitted, with appropriate precautions, only if this is expressly required by the Congregation.

Since it will contribute greatly to a more careful and expeditious solution of cases, it is hoped that copies of all judicial acts and documents will be typed and that the individual pages of the process, numbered and bound in a folder, will be guaranteed as to integrity and authenticity, with the certification of the actuary or notary of their faithful transcription.

## III  CLAUSES ATTACHED TO RESCRIPTS

After the pontifical dissolution of the bond of a non-consummated marriage has been granted, it is proper for the spouses to enter new marriages, provided this has not been prohibited. Such a prohibition may be expressed in two ways: an *ad mentem* clause (and in this case the *mens* can be of different kinds and is appropriately explained) or a *vetitum* clause.

a) The clause with the words *ad mentem,* which is prohibitory, is usually added when the fact of non-consummation depends on reasons of lesser significance, its removal is entrusted to the bishop, so that he may provide more suitably for pastoral needs. The bishop should not permit the remarriage of the party who asks for the removal of the clause unless after the prescribed regulations have been observed, the party is found to be truly ready to undertake the burdens of marriage and has promised that in the future he will fulfill his matrimonial duties in an honest and Christian manner.

b) In special cases, however, when the reason for non-consummation is a physical or psychic defect of major significance and seriousness, a *vetitum* for remarriage may be attached. Unless it so states in the rescript, this is not a diriment impediment but only a prohibiting impediment, the removal of which is reserved to the Apostolic See. Permission to remarry is granted if the petitioner, after making a petition to the Congregation and fulfilling the prescribed conditions, is shown to be capable of properly performing conjugal acts,

It is left to the bishop's judgement and pastoral consideration to inform the party with whom the second marriage is to be entered concerning either clause added to the rescript and later removed.

**DOCUMENT IV:**     Special Instruction of the Congregation for
the Doctrine of the Faith concerning the
procedure of natural bond cases, dated 6
December 1973.
(Ref: SCDF prot. no. 2717/68)

As is well known, this Congregation has subjected to lengthy
investigation and study the question of the dissolution of marriage
in favour of the faith.

At length, after this careful investigation, His Holiness, Pope
Paul VI, has approved new norms which express the conditions for
the grant of the dissolution of marriage in favour of the faith
whether the petitioner is baptised or converted or not.

I.        The following three conditions *sine qua non* are required for
the valid grant of the dissolution:

        a) absence of baptism in one of the spouses throughout the
entire period of conjugal life;

        b) non-use of marriage after baptism, if the sacrament is
received by the party who was previously non-baptised;

        c) that the unbaptised person or the person baptized
outside the Catholic Church leave to the Catholic party the freedom
and opportunity to profess his or her own religion and to baptise
and bring up the children as Catholics. This condition, in the form
of a promise *(cautio)*, is to be kept safely.

II.       The following are required in addition:
        §1. That there be no possibility of restoring conjugal life,
in view of the continuing radical and incurable separation.

        §2. That there be no danger of public scandal or serious
wonderment from the grant of the favour.

        §3. That the petitioner be shown not to have been the
culpable cause of the failure of a legitimate marriage and that the
Catholic party, with whom the new marriage is to be contracted or
validated, was not the guilty cause of the separation of the spouses.

        §4. That the second party in the prior marriage be
questioned, if possible, and not be reasonably opposed to the
granting of the dissolution.

§5. That the party who seeks the dissolution sees to the religious formation of any children from the prior marriage.

§6. That equitable provision be made, according to the norms of justice, for the previous spouse and any children.

§7. That the Catholic party with whom the new marriage is to be entered lives in accord with his or her baptismal promises and is concerned for the welfare of the new family.

§8. If it is a question of a catechumen with whom marriage is to be contracted, there should be moral certainty of the baptism which is to be received in the future, if the baptism itself has not taken place (which is preferable).

III. The dissolution is more easily granted where there is a serious doubt concerning the validity of the marriage, arising on other grounds.

IV. It is also possible to dissolve the marriage between a Catholic and an unbaptised person which was entered into with a dispensation from the impediment of disparity of cult, provided the conditions established in nos. II and III are verified and it is established that the Catholic, because of the particular circumstances of the region, especially the small number of Catholics, could not have avoided marriage and lead a life proper to the Catholic religion in that marriage. It is necessary, in addition that this Congregation be informed concerning the public knowledge of the marriage celebrated.

V. The dissolution of a legitimate marriage entered into with a dispensation from the impediment of disparity of cult is not granted to a Catholic petitioner in order to enter a new marriage with an unbaptised person who is not converted.

VI. The dissolution of a legitimate marriage which was contracted or validated after a dissolution from a previous legitimate marriage is not granted.

In order that these conditions may be properly fulfilled, new procedural norms have been drawn up, and all future processes are to be carried out in accord with them. These norms are attached to the present Instruction.

With the establishment of the new norms, the earlier regulations for the conduct of these processes are entirely abrogated.

## PROCEDURAL NORMS FOR THE PROCESS OF DISSOLUTION OF THE BOND OF MARRIAGE IN FAVOUR OF THE FAITH

Art. 1 :    The process which is to precede the granting of the favour of a dissolution of a legitimate marriage is conducted by the local Ordinary who is competent in accord with the prescription of the Apostolic Letter *Causas Matrimoniales*. IV, §1, either personally or through another ecclesiastic delegated by him. The Acts to be sent to the Holy See must contain proof of the fact of delegation or commission.

Art. 2 :    Allegations must not be simply asserted but proved in accord with the prescriptions of the canon law, either by documents or by trustworthy depositions of witnesses.

Art. 3.     Both original documents and authentic copies must be certified by the Ordinary or by the delegated judge.

Art. 4 :    §1 In the preparation of questions to be asked of the parties and witnesses, the services of the defender of the bond or of some other person delegated for this function in individual cases must be employed. This delegation is to be mentioned in the Acts.

§2 Before the witnesses are questioned they must take an oath to speak the truth.

§3 The Ordinary or his delegate should ask the questions already prepared. He may add other questions which he judges appropriate for a better understanding of the matter or which are suggested by the responses already given.

When the parties or witnesses testify concerning facts not of their own knowledge, the judge should question them also concerning the reason for or the origin of their knowledge.

§4. The judge must take great care that the question and the responses be accurately transcribed by the notary and signed by the witnesses.

Art. 5 :    §1. If a non-Catholic witness refuses to present himself or to testify before a Catholic priest, a document containing a deposition on the matter given by the witness before a notary public or other trustworthy person may be accepted. This is to be expressly noted in the Acts.

§2. In order to decide whether this document is to be given credence, the Ordinary or the delegated judge should introduce sworn witnesses, especially Catholics, who know the non-Catholic witness well and are willing and able to testify to his truthfulness.

§3. The judge himself should also express his opinion concerning the credence to be given to this document.

Art. 6:   §1. The absence of baptism in one of the spouses is to be demonstrated in such a way that all prudent doubt is removed.

§2. The party who says that he was baptised should be questioned under oath, if possible.

§3. Moreover, witnesses and especially the parents and blood relatives of the party should be examined, as well as others, especially those who knew the party during infancy or throughout the course of his life.

§4. Witnesses are to be questioned not only concerning the absence of baptism but also concerning the circumstances which make it believable or probable that baptism was not conferred.

§5. Care should be taken to search the baptismal registers of places where the person who was said to be unbaptised lived during infancy, especially in churches which he frequented to acquire religious instruction or where the marriage was celebrated.

Art. 7:   §1. If at the time the dissolution is sought the unbaptised person has already been admitted to baptism, at least a summary process must be conducted, with the intervention of the defender of the bond, concerning the non-use of marriage after reception of baptism.

§2. The party should be questioned under oath concerning the kind of contract he or she may have had with the other party after the separation and especially asked whether following baptism he or she had matrimonial relations with the other person.

§3. The other party is also to be questioned, under oath if possible, concerning the non-consummation of the marriage.

§4. In addition, witnesses, especially blood relatives and friends, are to be questioned, likewise under oath, not only concerning what has taken place after the separation of the parties and especially after the baptism, but also with regard to the probity and truthfulness of the parties, that is, concerning the credence which their testimony deserves.

Art. 8:   The petitioner, if converted and baptised, should be questioned concerning the time and the intention which led him to receive baptism or to be converted.

Art. 9: §1. In the same case, the judge should question the parish priest and other priests who participated in the doctrinal instruction and in the preparation for conversion concerning the reason which led the petitioner to receive baptism.

§2. The Ordinary should never direct any petition to the Congregation for the Doctrine of the Faith unless every reasonable suspicion concerning the sincerity of conversion has been removed.

Art. 10: §1. The Ordinary or judge should question the petitioner or the witnesses concerning the reason for the separation or divorce, namely, whether the petitioner was the cause or not.

§2. The judge should include in the Acts an authentic copy of the divorce decree.

Art. 11: The judge or the Ordinary should report whether the petitioner has children from the marriage or other union and how he has provided or intends to provide for their religious upbringing.

Art. 12: The judge or the Ordinary should likewise report how the petitioner will make or intends to make equitable provision for the spouse and the children if any, in accord with the laws of justice.

Art. 13: The Ordinary or judge should gather information concerning the non-Catholic party from whom he may determine whether the restoration of conjugal life can be hoped for. He should not fail to report whether the non-Catholic party has attempted a new marriage after divorce.

Art. 14: The Ordinary should report expressly whether any danger is to be feared of scandal, *admiratio,* or calumnious interpretation if the dissolution were to be granted, either among Catholics or among non-Catholics, as if the Church in practice was favourable to divorce. He should explain the circumstances which makes this danger probable in the case or exclude it.

Art. 15: The Ordinary should express the reasons which support the granting of the favour in the individual cases, at the same time always adding whether the petitioner has already attempted a new marriage in any form or is living in another union. The Ordinary should also report the fulfilment of the conditions for the grant of the favour and whether the promises mentioned in no. I, c), were

given. He should transmit an authentic document, with
these promises.

Art. 16:     The Ordinary should send to the Congregation for the
Doctrine of the Faith three copies of the petition, all the
Acts, and the information concerning which he is bound
to report.

# INDEX